PRAISE FO

"This book is a must-read for spiritual formation. Larry Smith clearly understands and articulates that sanctification is not simply about behavioral modification but spiritual transformation. In a world where so many of our leaders are failing due to a lack of character and integrity, the upward, inward and outward model gives us a Christ-centered blueprint for becoming and remaining faithful to the call our Lord Jesus Christ gave us to follow Him."

—Larry L. Anderson Jr.
Director of Church Health BRN PA/SJ
Senior Pastor of Great Commission Church
Adjunct Professor at Biblical Theological Seminary

"A must-read for every person who desires to be a true disciple of Christ; whether a seasoned church leader or a new believer, this book will teach, challenge and inspire. Most of all it will bring you back to the centrality of our existence—Jesus Christ. In a complicated and confusing world, Larry Smith shows the path back to the simple, yet profound, core of our faith, a life centered on Christ. This is a book to read over and over."

—Dr. Coz Crosscombe
Director of Urban Ministry First Year Programs
Cairn University

"In this book, Pastor Larry Smith equips believers to experience the beauty of living with Jesus as the center of our daily lives. He demonstrates how that commitment strengthens and enhances our relationships with others and transforms our knowledge of ourselves. I love how he points out self-awareness as an important aspect of spiritual maturity. *Jesus Life* is a must-read and will be a great resource for our leadership team."

—Jerome Gay
Lead Pastor, Vision Church
Raleigh, NC

"Having served two decades in pastoral ministry, my friend Larry Smith gives us a refreshingly practical, theologically precise tool that will guide us to re-center our affections firmly in Christ. *Jesus Life* will aid us to view the essence of the gospel as the foundation for all life and ministry as it places Christ in vivid, high definition."

—Doug Logan, Jr.
Lead Pastor, Epiphany Fellowship
Camden, NJ

"This is a must-read book for every believer who desires to be like Christ in all of life. Indeed there are so many things that seek to replace the position of Christ in our daily life. Larry Smith has written the very practical and profound truth that will help Christians across every culture to live a Christ-centered life."

—Robert Manda
Senior Pastor, Eastern Light Presbyterian Church
President, Pastoral Training Institute
Malawi, Africa

"Larry Smith has written a work that has been actually utilized and shaped in the crucible of real ministry, not in the ivory tower of theory. Any pastor, leader, or, disciple maker would benefit from this book and use it as a resource for their personal commitment to the Great Commission and spiritual formation. Please add it to your repertoire for becoming a more effective disciple and to make more disciples."

—Dr. Eric Mason
Founder & Lead Pastor, Epiphany Fellowship
Author of *Manhood Restored,*
Beat God to the Punch and *Unleashed*

"So many books on the Christian life reduce it to believing in a certain theology and submitting to a set of rules. The problem with this is that if theology and rules were all that sinners need, Jesus would have never had to come. God's greatest and best gift to sinners is Himself in the person and work of Jesus. Because this is true, the Christian life is about knowing, loving, serving and worshiping Jesus. I am thankful that this book not only makes this clear, but unpacks exactly what it means to give yourself to a Jesus-centric way of living."

—Dr. Paul Tripp
Best-selling Author

JESUS LIFE

JESUS LIFE

CONNECTED LIVING IN A DISCONNECTED WORLD

LARRY SMITH

CLC
PUBLICATIONS
Fort Washington, PA 19034

Jesus Life
Published by CLC Publications

U.S.A.
P.O. Box 1449, Fort Washington, PA 19034

UNITED KINGDOM
CLC International (UK)
51 The Dean, Alresford, Hampshire, SO24 9BJ

Printed in the United States of America.

ISBN (paperback): 978-1-61958-201-9
ISBN (e-book): 978-1-61958-202-6

Italicized words in Scripture quotes are the emphasis of the author.

CONTENTS

PART ONE

PART TWO

FOREWORD

Anyone who knows my ministry well knows the phrases that I often use. One of them is Christ-first versus Christ-centered. In Colossians 1:15-20, Paul displays a lofty view of Jesus. One of the things that He communicates is that Jesus is given first place by God the Father in all things. The idea of Jesus being first also points to Him being central. Paul further drives home this idea by stating that Jesus Christ holds everything seen and unseen in creation together. In other words, He is the sustainer of all things.

Our lives as believers are on an ever-flowing trajectory of making Jesus Christ central in our practical living. In order to grow in Christ, we must be graciously consumed with this. In being consumed, we must also constantly discern whether or not our eyes are being fixed on the Author and Finisher of our faith. God is always at work, working and willing His good pleasure in us. Our faith must be driven by His glorious initiative toward all of the movements in our lives.

This is why this book, *Jesus Life*, is so important. I have watched Larry Smith work this reality out on many practical levels of his life. He has been committed to engaging these truths in his family, in the local church and in his own life. Now the broader church will experience this transformative reality from his needed voice.

I am so glad to see that *Jesus Life* is about the comprehensive work of God through the Spirit who does what only He can do.

He works on the deepest levels of our lives, constantly conforming us to the image of Jesus Christ. When you read *Jesus Life* you will experience a practical resource that is biblically rich and frontline tested. Your journey will be strengthened by Jesus as he erases the identity confusion in your soul so that you are fully and truly found in Him.

—Dr. Eric Mason
Founder and Lead Pastor of Epiphany Fellowship
Author of *Manhood Restored,*
Beat God to the Punch and *Unleashed*

ACKNOWLEDGEMENTS

This book represents not only my own work and thought but also the faithfulness of many mentors, teachers, and pastors who have discipled me in Jesus over the years. I cannot and will not try to thank everyone here because I would, undoubtedly, forget some who have had important influences on my life.

There are two men who stand out among those who took me under their wings while I was still a baby Christian. Pastor Charles Brown, Jr. and Pastor Charles Minor are godly men whose investment in me has forever shaped my soul. These men stamped deeply into my heart a love for the Word of God. Though I was not aware of it at the time, the time I spent at each of their homes, whether watching a ball game, eating, or being destroyed at Ping-Pong (I am still in recovery, Pastor Minor) was instrumental in Christ being formed in me.

I am also greatly indebted to my family at Epiphany Fellowship Church. Being a part of a church that takes seriously the "one-anothers" of Scripture has been an enormous blessing in my life. Our lead pastor, Dr. Eric Mason, along with my fellow pastors, Nyron Burke, Curtis Dunlap, Tommy Forester, and Doug Logan have consistently challenged me and inspired me to serve God with integrity and diligence.

Pastor Robert Manda, from Malawi, Africa, has blessed me beyond words. In the last several years, through our partnership and your vision for planting Christ-centered churches in

Africa, I have seen the powerful and inspiring commitment of a man with a true servant's heart. Your faithfulness and integrity have helped hone my understanding of what it means to walk with God.

Finally, I have had a partner over the last thirty years who has taught me more about walking with Jesus than anyone else. When I struggle with what it looks like to be faithful to God and to walk with Him through hardship, I can simply look at my wife, Harriette. She has been a great rock for me through the years and has patiently endured my messiness as the Lord has been at work, slowly making me more like Jesus. Her consistent love, especially when I have been unlovely, has been a great tutor in helping me to know Christ.

I am thankful for all of the friends who have helped me through the years to see Jesus more clearly. Thank you Dave Almack of CLC Publications for taking a chance on me as a first-time author. I also want to thank my editor, Erika Cobb, who has done so much through her questions and comments to bring this book to life. Thanks to everyone at CLC who has worked on this project to bring it to completion.

INTRODUCTION

I vividly remember as a young believer wanting to learn the "secret" of the Christian life. I was a nineteen-year-old freshmen in college who had grown up in a religious family but had just come to know Jesus for the first time. I wanted to please Him. I wanted my life to count for God. I wanted to be a great Christian. I was becoming aware of just how sinful I was and how much I needed God's power at work in my life. I desperately wanted to have a life that showed off the power of God (and made me look like a real "star").

I remember reading Jesus' words in John 15: 7. "If you abide in me, and my words abide in you, *ask whatever you wish, and it will be done for you.*" Although the whole passage emphasizes abiding in Christ, I was focused on the "ask whatever you wish" part. I just knew that there was something—some special prayer, or some secret key that could deliver me into a new realm of the Christian life. Looking back, I see the error of my thoughts and this is what this book is about. Through many painful experiences that were the result of my own self-centeredness, God has patiently and consistently directed me back to Jesus. The emphasis of my Christianity was me—and God does not put up with that for long!

Before anything else we say about the Christian life, we must first say that it is about Jesus Christ. Jesus is the basic and ever-present reality that defines the life of every believer. This is hardly groundbreaking news to any spiritually mature believer, but it is the continual life-defining challenge of every Christian. Bombarded by the unholy trinity of the world, the flesh and the devil, the Christian is confronted with the temptation to make something else, anything else, the central focus of life. It does not matter if that focus is good (marriage, family, church or career) or evil (addictions, pride or materialism). The prime directive of all enemy forces is one thing: Replace Jesus.

The Enemy encourages us to replace Jesus as the center of our affections. Subtly, he entices us to replace Jesus as the center of our worship and relationships. Soon our very thoughts become: Help me find glory in something besides Jesus. *Help me construe a meaningful identity apart from Jesus. Help me make it, someway, somehow, in somebody's eyes, without the crutch of Christ defining me.*

UNTANGLING THE LIE

This lie is as old as Genesis 3. The serpent tells Eve that God is holding back from her and Adam. He tells her that eating from the Tree of the Knowledge of Good and Evil will make them just like God (3:4–5). In his crafty way he insinuates that God does not want what is best for them and so they need to eat of the forbidden fruit in order to get the life that God is holding back from them. This is the same lie he has been shoveling out ever since. The Enemy of your soul wants you to believe that there is life apart from Jesus—THERE IS NOT!

Jesus was not speaking hyperbolically in John 15:5 when He said, "apart from me you can do nothing." He was not speaking hyperbolically, but He was speaking factually. There is nothing that you or I will ever do that will bring glory to God that does not find its root and source in the person and work of Jesus

Christ. In fact, anything we do, no matter how moral, noble or seemingly excellent, amounts to less than nothing in God's eyes if it is not "rooted and grounded" in Christ (see Eph. 3:16–17). Scripture makes that abundantly clear book after book, chapter after chapter and verse after verse. The very definition of a righteous man, from a biblical perspective, is rooted in what he believes, through faith, and not simply in what he does.

Old Testament prophet Habakkuk wrote, "But the righteous shall live by his faith" (Hab. 2:4). It is true that the works of the righteous (or the fruit as the Bible often describes it) follow after and conform to their faith. But this is just the point. Faith in Jesus informs, undergirds and infuses the life of the believer in such a way that it leads to "good fruit." I remember how faith informed me when I was leaving my first pastorate, feeling like a failure, with no job prospects and a young family. Faith allowed me to make a difficult and right decision to resign, believing that somehow the Lord was not finished with me. Faith undergirds and strengthens my wife and me every day as we pray for people and situations that never seem to change.

Over thirty years ago my wife and I began to pray for her brother Ralph. He was a crack addict, in and out of jail, and did not seem to be making any progress. Faith kept us on our knees. Some years later Ralph's life changed drastically through a powerful encounter with the Lord Jesus Christ. Today Ralph is the husband of a godly wife, an ordained minister and a trustworthy man. He is one of the most godly men I know. There is nothing that I have that I would not trust him with. Faith undergirds believers to continue to look to God even when the evidence of our senses says it is useless.

MODERN DAY IDOLOTRY

The human heart is an idol factory. One sorry consequence of the sin of our first parents, Adam and Eve, is that every human heart disconnected from God desperately attempts to find life and meaning apart from God. Idolatry is the use of anything or anyone to take the place of God. We commonly make idols of money, relationships, sex, health, fitness, body type, education, virtual friendships, popularity, and the list goes on. All of these things can be good if they are in their proper place. They become idols to us because we use them to become primary markers of identity and demand from them what God never intended for them to give us. The pathetic irony of sin is that we attempt to forge meaning, purpose, identity and joy apart from the only One who makes each of those things possible. And the "we" includes every one of us. Whether a preacher, a president, or a prostitute, we all find ourselves trying to forge an identity where we are the center.

But God, the lover of our souls, will not allow it. As creator He holds rights over us as His creatures. As sustainer He alone works in such a way that life is enabled to continue day by day. As redeemer He is the only One whose love is so great that He takes upon Himself the punishment that we rightly deserve for our sin and rebellion, and credits us with His righteous perfection (see 2 Cor. 5:21). And we look for life somewhere else . . . anywhere else . . . foolishness!

When Eve started looking at that fruit and saw it as something desirable—in that instant it became an idol to her. God was no longer enough. If we are not careful we can do the same thing with an iPhone, a flat screen, a job promotion, or a relationship. Whenever we need something that we don't really need, it is a sure sign that we have moved into idolatry. I remember being well trained in this as a child watching cartoons on Saturday mornings. Being bombarded with commercials about the latest toys, I was easily driven to a desperate place of contrived need. The same inflamed desire that burned as idolatry to me as a six-year-old easily resurfaces almost fifty years later.

I am writing this because awareness of these realities, however helpful it might be, does not stop the idol factory from putting out its product. Though we may give intellectual assent to these truths, knowledge does almost nothing apart from a radically transformed heart. It does little to extinguish the fire of lust for a meaningful and satisfying life apart from *complete dependence on Jesus Christ.*

In some ways, the Western church, with its great bastions of theological education and rich history of biblical exposition, finds itself in great danger. We have become top heavy with knowledge but very inefficient in adopting a lifestyle that resembles what we say we believe. Two popular cartoon characters perfectly provide an illustration of this imbalance. Charlie Brown, from the *Peanuts* comic strip, has an extra-large head that is out of balance with the rest of his body. Olive Oyl, from the *Popeye* comic strip, has the skinniest body possible. Now, imagine a character with a Charlie Brown head and an Olive Oyl body. This image demonstrates how we are of proportion with a "head" (or theological knowledge), that makes us think we are something. Our body, however, does not have the strength to carry out the "knowledge" that we are so proud to possess. The gap between what we "know" about God and how we actually live only widens. Our Charlie Brown head falls to the ground because our Olive Oyl body just can't hold it up.

THE DISCONNECTED SOUL

It is often comfortable to talk about the Western church in such terms but the analogy needs to be personalized. I am growing more and more aware of the disconnect within my own soul. I can spout the doctrines of grace and proclaim the freedom of forgiveness that comes from the finished work of Christ. Just a few days ago, I remember speaking eloquently about how God is able to remove the guilt of our sin in the very moment that we turn to Him in repentance. Later the same day, I found myself disgusted and lost in my anger with a friend who had fallen *again* into sin. He had reached out to me to confess and repent, but in my heart my anger seethed because he just wasn't making progress fast enough for me! Theoretically, I glory in the truth of Romans 8:1, "There is therefore now no condemnation for those who are in Christ Jesus," but realistically I only apply that truth according to the moods and predilections of my own fickle heart. God help me in my hypocrisy!

With all of this in mind, this book is designed to help you comprehensively build your life around abiding in Jesus Christ. Your flesh (or sinful nature) will continue to resist the lordship of Christ and your need to depend upon Him until you die. God's work of justification and even sanctification does not alter the characteristic nature of our flesh. Our flesh is always self-centered, always greedy, and never satisfied. The writer of Ecclesiastes describes the reality of the flesh when he says, "the eye is not satisfied with seeing, nor the ear filled with hearing" (Eccles. 1:8). Only in glorification, when we receive a new body that is consistent with that of Jesus Christ's resurrection body, will we experience perfect continuity as whole people who love God rightly. Therefore we are in the fight of a lifetime, to destroy the idol factories of our hearts and set up Jesus Christ alone as the One we worship and cling to with all of our being.

WHERE WE ARE GOING

This book is arranged in three sections that detail three areas of spiritual movement that enable us to comprehensively make Jesus Christ the center of our lives. I use the word "movement" to describe the fact there is a dynamic, conscious, and purposeful thrust that powerfully propels us forward in our relationship with God. Before going into these movements, chapter 1 lays out our problem in more detail. The roots and shoots of the idolatry we have talked about are attempting to thwart every effort to grow in intimate relationship with Jesus. Why is it that we continue to seek life outside of relationship with God? Why do we think that we can actually find life apart from Jesus?

The first movement is the upward movement whereby we focus on God Himself and allow His glory to transform us. In the second movement, the inward movement, we become increasingly aware of who we actually are in Christ and comprehend both our present reality and our promised future. The final section of the book is called, "The Outward Movement." This details how believers are called to live in community with other believers and called to have a lifestyle of sharing their faith in Christ with those who do not know Him.

My prayer is that this book will help you to desire Christ more passionately, to know Christ more deeply and to serve Christ more fervently. To experience the embrace of God, whose love for you is not based on anything you have done, is the promised destination of believers. As the movements of your life converge to make Jesus Christ the center of all that you are and all that you value, you will experience the promised rest that God has secured for you by the finished work of Jesus Christ. You can truly experience Jesus Life.

1

JESUS REPLACEMENTS

Sometimes when I listen to people who say they have lost their faith, I am far less surprised than they expect. If their view of God is what they say, then it is only surprising that they did not reject it much earlier.

—Os Guinness

I will never forget that day—that moment. Looking across a crowded room at a party I saw my wife for the first time. Now don't get me wrong, I'd seen Harriette many times before. We went to church together, we taught Sunday school together, and we even worked with the youth group together. I had seen her many times before but this time was different—drastically different.

In a flash, I thought, "This could be my wife!" I was a twenty-two-year-old young buck without a real clue. We had not dated or even talked about the possibility of relationship but this young lady had somehow captured my heart. And with this I began to reorient my thinking and my actions so that I could get to see her, to get to know her, and to get to talk with her. I was scared, excited, nervous, not ready and ready all at the same time. All of a sudden getting close to her meant so much more to me than missing the first quarter of a football game! I can remember taking her out for the first time and holding her hand.

My hand began sweating profusely and I had to keep wiping if off on my jeans. It was a little bit funny, a lot embarrassing, and I did not care. I was simply exhilarated by the prospect of getting to know Harriette better and hoping that it would lead us to marriage.

A deep longing to be near. Doesn't that describe the essence of love? Have you ever witnessed a gray-haired couple with wrinkles and a halted gait gently holding hands and staring at one another with delight? You might expect it from the young because they have not known each other long enough to see past the façade of contrived care to understand the depth of sin and selfishness in their partner. For that matter, the young are not yet aware of the degree of their own shallow reservoir of genuine love that sits atop a Marianas Trench of selfish ambition. But the elderly couple, the aged man and wife, have seen and experienced it. Their tender touch and loving gaze means more—much more. It means that somewhere and somehow below the depths of leaking sin there is a sure and strong hope. It means that there is a power at work far greater than any natural force known to mankind. It means that God is actively involved with His created loved ones, to forgive and to restore and to love with a resilient and potent love that will not be stopped.

While many Christian writers have rightly warned us that love is not primarily an emotion or feeling, we must also be careful never to go to the other extreme. Made in the image and likeness of God, human beings were never made to robotically progress through a series of tests which will prove the genuineness of their love. Much the opposite. In fact, the proper completion of any task, no matter how noble, difficult or "godly," has little to do with the state of the heart. We can complete a task with excellence and yet our hearts can be far from God.

God always goes deeper and requires us to do the same. Robotic obedience to His law has never been His aim. Jesus quoted from Isaiah in denouncing the Pharisees legalistic but dead-hearted obedience. "This people honors me with their lips, but their heart is far from me" (Matt. 15:8). God's interest lies not in what is observable to the naked eye, but He consumes Himself with "piercing to the division of soul and spirit, of joints and marrow, and discerning the thoughts and intentions of the heart" (Heb. 4:12). And so He calls us to a love that transforms from the inside out: an outward obedience directed by an inward longing.

Even as we acknowledge that truth, our preoccupation with performance and results often chokes us in a near-death grip. I recently had a conversation with a friend. As I talked with him his frustration grew and grew. He was mad at God (but he would not say those words). He would say that he was disappointed and confused. He deeply desired freedom from a sinful preoccupation that he could not shake. His disappointment and frustration came from the fact that although he prayed earnestly to God for deliverance, God did not come through. Though there may have been some minor victories, a fuller vantage point of the battlefield revealed a pattern of progress in the negative. "If only God would help me with this one thing," he complained, "I would serve him well and depend upon him fully."

This is a chorus I hear over and over again in pastoral work. To be honest, I hear it often in my own mind. But this mindset gets to the heart of the struggle. We demand a sovereign act of power from God to set us free from our sin and weakness and then declare that if He does it we will depend upon him. We say, "I want to live a life of dependence from a position of strength." God does not work that way. He never has and He never will.

GETTING TO THE HEART

Consider this: Setting you free from your outward struggle with sin is not God's primary goal in your life. God is not preoccupied with your perfection. Let's face it, if He was He would be constantly frustrated and agitated. The redeeming Lord of the universe is not obsessing about your addictions and sin tendencies. There never has been and there never will be an emergency meeting of the Trinity because you can't break your bad habit. It is simply not on the top of His list.

If that is true that then we might ask, "What is on the top of His list?" Simply this: *that you might know Him*. As John 17:3 says, "And this is eternal life, that they know you the only true God, and Jesus Christ whom you have sent." This is not the knowledge of the halls of academia but the knowledge of the wedding hall. It is less like boardroom knowledge and more like bedroom knowledge. It is the knowing of the other at the most intimate level. This is God's invitation; this is God's command; and this is God's preoccupation.

God wants you to know Him. He wants you to experience Him. He invites you to a relationship of reciprocal knowledge. Psalm 139 describes the depth of the knowledge that God has of you. He knows when you sit down or rise up (139:2). He knows what you are thinking before you say it (139:4). He has fixed things in such a way that whatever you do, you cannot get away from Him (139:7-12). He formed you in your mother's womb; and even before creation, He knew what every day of your life would look like (139:13-16). Therefore, the plain truth of Scripture from Genesis to Revelation is this: He wants you to know Him with that same type of intimacy!

It is not an outward conformity to His law that He is preoccupied with, but a reciprocal knowledge between groom and bride. This age does not end with a graduation ceremony but with a marriage celebration (see Rev. 19:6–8). We do not graduate with a PhD in Jesusology, but we become a part of the eternal bride of Christ (see 2 Cor. 11:2). Time and creation under the governance of God moves steadily toward the full revelation of the person of God with unbridled clarity. God moves all things toward that day when "the earth is filled with the knowledge of the glory of God as the waters cover the sea" (Hab. 2:14).

It is within the confines of this intimate relationship that sin loosens its grip on your new heart because it is now overwhelmed by that which is more compelling than sin ever was—a clear view of God. Legalistic observance of the law can never free a heart from the strangling grip of sin. Only in an ever-deepening relationship with the person of Jesus, where we begin to recognize His glory and beauty, is the grasp of sin forcibly removed from the believer's neck. True freedom is given when we begin to comprehend the grandeur of the revelation of God's love for us.

THE DEMONSTRATION OF GOD'S LOVE

The pivotal moment of this revelation has already occurred. It happened over two thousand years ago when a baby was born in a seemingly insignificant town in a district far removed from the halls of power of the Roman government that ruled with a strong hand. A little boy was born to a young woman, a virgin, betrothed to a man but not yet sexually involved. The Bible tells us that the Holy Spirit came upon young Mary so that the second person of the Godhead, the Eternal Son, was conceived in her womb. The Timeless God, who himself, created all things, took on an additional nature, and became a man.

In the most profound of all mysteries, God took on this new nature as a man in order that He might save those whom He loves. Though they did not love Him and though the hands that He created would drive the nails through His hands and feet, and the mouths that He created would curse Him, He came to save them. Though each of us is full of sin and desires our own comfort above God's glory, He came to save us. Jesus came into a world that suffers under the curse of sin and the judgment of God (see Gen. 3:17–19). Jesus left behind the eternal blessedness of His divine position to experience the fullness of the human condition in a world under the curse. And in doing so He Himself became a curse for us so that He might redeem us from the curse that we rightly deserve (see Gal. 3:13–14).

Let's stop and meditate for a moment. While unbelievers may mock the mystery that they cannot understand, believers often fly too quickly past the foundation that all life springs from. But this is the problem. There is no life apart from Jesus Christ. Understood rightly, all life flows from connection to the creator, sustainer and redeemer of life—Jesus who is the Christ. Certainly there is an appearance of life apart from Christ, but just as certainly, this "life" does not exist.

THE ILLUSION OF "LIFE"

Some years ago I watched in amazement as the magician David Copperfield performed a trick where the Statue of Liberty disappeared before the eyes of thousands of onlookers as well as millions of people watching on television. Now the Statue of Liberty sits in the middle of New York Harbor, is over three hundred feet high and can be seen from Manhattan, Brooklyn, Staten Island and New Jersey. How could this massive object, planted on an island in the middle of the harbor and visible to millions, simply vanish? Although I knew that what I was witnessing was an illusion, my senses told me otherwise. Seeing is believing after all. To the amazement of everyone, including myself, Copperfield was able to engage the audience in a sensory experience in such a way that what they knew was not possible looked and felt as if it were real.

And this is the illusion, the matrix if you will, in which we live. Even for believers our sensory experience of life does not need to include Jesus at all. *We can have what we define as life, even a good life, without the involvement of Jesus. He has become for many a nice add-on or a wonderful accessory but certainly not the substance of life itself.* A good job, financial security, a nice place to live, healthy children—all of these things can seem like the real substance of life. A prosperous life with minimal conflict can become the idolatrous goal and relationship with Jesus becomes a minor accessory. And this is exactly where we have lost our way and been deceived.

It was Jesus who declared, "I am the way, and the truth, and the life. No one comes to the Father except through me" (John 14:6). If our definition of life is in submission to God we must admit that life does not and cannot exist apart from Jesus Christ. Defining life in any other way, whether through accomplishments, happiness, riches, education or even building a lasting legacy, is antithetical to the truth. When we define life in this way we are in effect "swallowing the blue pill" that allows us to continue to live in a matrix of illusion. You have a critical choice to make that which will determine both the true quality of your life now and the degree of eternal reward that you will one day receive (see 1 Cor. 3:12–15).

Life is in Jesus—period. Believing this is the "red pill" of God-created reality. To the degree this is believed, experiencing real life becomes a possibility. To the degree that it is doubted—and your actions will reveal your doubts—you will miss what

God defines as life. You will miss out on experiencing a Jesus Life—one that abounds in the richness of God's promises and connects you to the source of all that is good and perfect.

Knowing and experiencing Jesus is life. He is the center around which everything else must revolve. Although creation declares the glory of God (see Ps. 19:1), a deep and saving knowledge of God requires knowing Jesus Christ (see John 17:3). Jesus is the final and perfect revelation of God to man. He is "the exact imprint of his nature" (Heb. 1:3) and the One in whom the "fullness of deity dwells bodily" (Col. 2:9).

GROWING TO KNOW JESUS

Though you may say a hearty "Amen" to the paragraph above, what is your life saying about this fact? If you believe that Jesus Christ is the Creator/Redeemer God-man, then how does your life reflect this? When you look at your schedule or consider your thought life or how you spend your money, is there a clear reflection that you believe that true life can only be found in Jesus? Or would you see a great deal of inconsistency and a struggle to find life in a multitude of other things? Our struggle as believers is to grow in a lifestyle that is consumed with knowing Jesus Christ personally and intimately. We want to live in such a way that He becomes our first priority, our central reality and our deepest desire.

The truth of the matter is that just knowing this or agreeing with the statement is not enough. In the thirty-five years since I surrendered my life to Jesus Christ as a college freshmen, I have not walked this way consistently. With a thousand stops and starts, I have grown to know him better. Sometimes when I have wanted to give up I just could not. After experiencing heartbreaking pain and betrayal by leaders in the church, at one point

I desired to leave the church altogether. When I have become discouraged with my own lack of progress or the failure to make any real difference for God in this world, I have wanted to just throw in the towel on ministry and go sell plumbing supplies somewhere. Thanks be to God for His powerful love that keeps us, encourages us, and draws us to Himself!

Just what is it that keeps us from a consistent lifestyle that centers on Jesus? First and foremost the enemy is our flesh. This does not mean simply our physical body (remember Jesus himself has a physical body) but our inherited nature of sin that is bent away from God. The sinful nature that we all share is that deep urge that causes us to put our comfort and pleasure above God's glory and the good of our neighbor. In order to do this, even as believers, we need to suppress the truth that God is always making plain to us, and decide to serve self instead of Jesus.

Paul describes the unrighteousness of humanity as "suppressing the truth" (Rom. 1:18). When I think of this verse the image I have is that of submerging a beach ball under water. Because of the air in the ball and its buoyancy, it takes a great deal of force to keep the ball under water. In the same way because we are image bearers of God, His moral truth is etched into our conscious. Our sinful nature, however, constantly works to suppress God's truth so that we can live according to our selfish desires. Like the swimmer who must continually fight to keep the ball under the water, our sin nature fights to keep God's truth submerged so that we can do what is comfortable and pleasing to our flesh.

LIFE AS WORSHIP

Some years ago this truth became painfully evident to me. I had finished reading an outstanding Christian book that was written to help men overcome their battle with lust. The book was helpful and very practical, but I knew that I was missing something. Sometime later, while reading the book of Romans, I was deeply challenged by one particular verse. "I appeal to you therefore, brothers, by the mercies of God, to present your bodies as a living sacrifice, holy and acceptable to God, which is your spiritual worship" (Rom. 12:1). In a moment I saw the truth that I had been missing. My willingness to give myself over to lustful thoughts and ungodly affections was not merely an issue of willpower or of growing stronger in my faith—at the heart it was an issue of worship.

God's appeal in this verse is based on "the mercies of God" which Paul had outlined earlier in the book. By God's mercy He came for each of us who was lost in sin and committed to our own way. By God's mercy, Jesus died on behalf of sinful people. By God's mercy, Jesus took upon himself the punishment for our sin. By God's mercy, when we turn to Christ in repentance and faith, we are declared not guilty of our sins. Even more than this declaration that we are not guilty (justification), by God's mercy He is also at work in us to progressively conform us to His image (sanctification). At the end of all things the "mercies of God" that Paul calls us to remember also includes the reality that one day we will be totally freed from every vestige of sin and share in the eternal beauty of a redeemed creation with our great God at the center of all things (glorification). Before we are commanded to do anything in this verse, we are reminded that the motivation we need is rooted in the wondrous mercies of our redeeming God.

Based on this we are given a command, "to present your bodies as a living sacrifice, holy and acceptable to God." This is something that we are called to do as believers, but the last part of the verse gives us the context for this act. Paul says that presenting our bodies to God in this way is your reasonable service of worship (see Rom. 12:1, KJV). This was the moment that a tsunami of truth flooded my soul. What I do with my thought life and with my body is not merely an issue of self-control or discipline but it is an issue of worship. Let me make this plain: what I began to understand is that when I choose to give my thoughts or my bodily actions over to lust I am replacing Jesus as the center of my worship and worshiping an idol.

This is the heart of the battle to make Jesus central in our lives. Jesus gets replaced by someone or something else as the center of our worship. Whether that consists of sexual objects, material wealth, personal comfort, a preoccupation about what others think about me or anything else, it is that same issue—we have replaced Jesus as the center of our worship. We can even replace Jesus with "good things" like loving our wives, caring for our children, working for social justice or being an exemplary employee. If we are not careful we can replace Jesus with some arbitrary standard of Facebook likes for our newest post or the number of Twitter followers I gained this week. In the end if anything but Jesus takes center stage we are living in idolatry. It does not take long in reading through Old Testament history to understand that idolatry was the primary sin problem of the Israelite nation. When you begin to understand the nature of idolatry as the Bible describes it, you will quickly come to understand that idolatry is your major issue as well.

In the Old Testament, animal sacrifices were continually being made which pointed to the "once for all" sacrifice of Jesus Christ (see Heb. 10:10). In every case the animals were first killed and then put on the altar in order to be burned and "sacrificed" to God on behalf of the people. The call of God to believers, however, is to be "living sacrifices." This is our challenge and our blessing. When the bull was put on the altar he had no choice but to stay there because he had already been slain. Our call as "living sacrifices" is to stay on the altar even as the heat of the flames becomes more and more unbearable.

The fidelity of our faith is revealed as we are presented with a hundred decisions every day that beckon us to forsake true worship and instead serve self, comfort, and reputation. Left to ourselves we will not consistently pass these tests. However, as we will see in chapter five, believers are infused with the life of God through the Holy Spirit in order to live out this calling. Moment-by-moment, believers are called to resist the temptation to put anything or anyone in the place that God has reserved exclusively for Himself.

Now please don't expect to get much help with this from the world that you live in. The Enemy has stacked the deck against you so that it will often feel impossible. If you are like me at all, these forces will sometimes leave you discouraged, bewildered and perhaps even on the verge of giving up. The feeling of defeat does not mean that you are not a Christian—only that you are human. Like a salmon swimming against a strong current, a believer does not move towards Christ on a consistent basis without much effort and many bruises. But the good news is this: the imparted life of Jesus Christ in the life of a believer is more powerful than the instinct that draws the salmon back to its spawning grounds. As the salmon succeeds against all odds, so will those who surrender their lives to Jesus. God has willed it to be so (see John 10:27–28).

Of course, behind the corruption of our flesh and a fallen world that woos us away from devotion to Christ stands an

Enemy that comes to steal, kill and destroy (see 10:10). The devil and his host of fallen angels are also desperately at work to nullify the redeeming power of God in your life. He will come in a myriad of ways, even clothed "as an angel of light" (2 Cor. 11:14) to lead you away from Christ. He comes in "philosophy and empty deceit" (Col. 2:8), he comes in worldly wisdom (see 1 Cor. 3:19), and he consistently comes dressed in religious, even "Christian," garb.

Rather than making you doubt the genuineness of your walk with God, the Lord has designed even the discouragements to bring you closer to Him. Layer by layer, the God removes our pride, self-centeredness, entitlement and a thousand other vices to clothe us with pure garments. Pride is replaced by humility, self-centeredness by love, and entitlement by a grateful heart. And as we replace the garments of vice with the garments of virtue, we grow in the awareness that these new clothes are not our own but are given to us by Jesus Christ.

Any voices, even so-called Christian ones, that serve to make anything other than Jesus Christ central in your life are, in fact, leading you away from Christ. When your personal well-being and self-esteem are central, then Jesus Christ is not. It is for this reason that John warns the early church community with these words, "Beloved, do not believe every spirit, but test the spirits to see whether they are from God, for many false prophets have gone out into the world" (1 John 4:1). John was not talking about religious and philosophical voices that were in various parts of the Roman Empire but specifically those that were making their way right into the church! Religious and "spiritual" voices often present to believers the most appealing Jesus replacements because they look so much like the real thing.

Take a moment to consider your life. What are some of the things that have become Jesus replacements for you? At various times in my own life my family, my job and my ministry have eclipsed Jesus as my central affection—and this is always an ongoing battle. At the center of my failures has been my unglodly desire for my own comfort. In addition, my preoccupation with how I am seen by others has often replaced my desire to see God glorified through my life. All of these things, and many more, have served as idols in my life and have at times kept me from experiencing life in Jesus. The good news of the gospel however trumps my sin. I have been redeemed by the precious blood of Christ and He is glorified all the more as He patiently and skillfully delivers me and makes me more and more like Him.

In the next five chapters we will discover very practical ways that demonstrate how we can begin to build a life that centers itself on a relationship with Jesus Christ. This is not a message for a select group of Christians—for pastors, priests and "saints." This is a message for anyone who claims to know Jesus as his or her Lord and Savior. It is a message for anyone who desires to experience the fullness of life that God offers. It is a message for you!

Lord Jesus, I am aware that I have made little of You and much of myself. I have looked to many things to do for me what You alone have promised to do. I have effectively replaced You with people, possessions and dreams that have obscured Your place in my life.

Lord, I repent of my idolatry and I make it my aim to worship You with my life and with my lips. For the sake of Jesus Christ, I ask You to forgive my sins and to grant me a deep and true repentance as I come to You. I thank You, Father, for the work of Your Son and the presence of the Holy Spirit in my life. Strengthen me to walk with You in truth today so that Christ may be greatly glorified through my life.

PART ONE

THE UPWARD MOVEMENT

FINDING LIFE BY CONNECTING TO JESUS

Without the Way there is no going; without the Truth there is no knowing; without the Life there is no living.

—Thomas à Kempis

As a five-year-old I was somehow really impressed by the way my parents dealt with the mail. I remember that my parents taught me not to touch certain pieces of mail because they were "important pieces of paper." For some bizarre reason this phrase really connected with me. I thought that if these pieces of paper (probably bills!) were so important they must be worth money. If that was the case then I could make "important pieces of paper" and sell them to our neighbors. And so, along with my best friend James, I started my first entrepreneurial enterprise. We scribbled with crayons on sheets of white paper and went door-to-door attempting to sell our important pieces of paper. I honestly don't remember if we sold any, but looking back on that I realize that things that seem weighty and important really might not be.

Isn't this a strong tendency for most of us? Like a child who prefers a shiny penny over an old dollar bill, we often assign value to the wrong things. Discerning what is critical from what is trivial is one of life's most important tasks. This is especially true for believers who want to grow in relationship with Jesus. The problem is that so much of modern day "Christianity" is a neatly packaged self-help/feel-better message that has little to do with the true gospel message. D.A. Carson points this out powerfully as he exposes the thinking of the "three-dollar gospel."

> I would like to buy about three dollars worth of gospel, please. Not too much—just enough to make me happy, but not so much that I get addicted. I don't want so much gospel that I learn to really hate covetousness and lust. I certainly don't want so much that I start to love my enemies, cherish self-denial, and contemplate missionary service in some alien culture. I want ecstasy, not repentance; I want transcendence, not transformation. I would like to be cherished by some nice, forgiving, broad-minded people, but I myself don't want to love those from different races—especially if they smell. I would like enough gospel to make my family secure and my children well behaved, but not so much that I find my ambitions redirected or my giving too greatly enlarged. I would like about three dollars worth of gospel, please.[1]

THE THREE-DOLLAR GOSPEL

Jesus says that the kingdom of heaven is like a treasure of untold worth that a man finds. It is worth so much that he is willing to sell every other possession that he has in order that he might obtain this one treasure of untold worth (see Matt. 13:44). The means of entry into the kingdom of heaven is the gospel. Indeed, the most weighty, the most costly, and the most valuable thing that we will ever discover here on earth is the truth of the gospel.

And yet I am afraid that we have often come to get our gospel from the dollar store. We easily become content with something that has the adornments and accoutrements of the real thing, but conveniently, does not ask so much of us. We effortlessly fall into the trap of religion without even knowing it. If we perform the right rituals (going to church, reading our Bibles sometimes, perhaps involvement in some ministry or good work) then we can check off the list and continue to live life as we otherwise please. Service completed, list checked off, heart unchanged.

This describes the vast majority of "Christians" in most churches. Whether Protestant or Catholic, evangelical or liberal, fundamentalist or Pentecostal the formula stands up. The list of religious rituals might change from attending sacraments to speaking in tongues to feeding the homeless to attending "deep" Bible studies to not speaking in tongues, but the fundamental reality remains the same. "Christians" define themselves within their camp largely by attending to the specific rituals and duties that define that camp. Done fervently, completed reverently, lived out consistently this is still dollar store "Christianity."

REAL CHRISTIANITY—UNION WITH CHRIST

Of course the issue is a simple one. Fundamentally, Christianity is never defined by rituals or works but by being united to Jesus Christ. Union with Christ, not just as a theological proposition but as a daily life-defining reality, is at the heart of God's activity in creation and redemption. It is this union that Christ came to make a reality. It is this union that puts the glory of God on display in high definition.

Now as nice as this all sounds, it is actually an ugly and brutal truth—and that is why we so desperately desire to avoid it. I say ugly and brutal because union with the perfect and holy God requires that anything not like Him be exposed, destroyed and replaced. And there is a whole lot in me that is not like Him. I suspect the same is true of you.

Proper adherence to religion requires the ongoing execution of specific acts and duties. Union with Christ requires the ongoing *execution* of self. Did you catch that? The first use of execution refers to completing a task but the second use of execution refers to the killing of something—namely you! "I have been crucified with Christ," Paul cries out, "and I no longer live but Christ lives in me" (Gal. 2:20). Paul says in another place "I die daily" (1 Cor. 15:31). What do these phrases mean? In context it is abundantly clear—the life of Jesus within me is constantly causing me to put to death those things that are not like Him. This is not a twelve-step program or forty days to a healthier you; this is the ongoing work of the Holy Spirit in the life of a believer guided by God's word to be conformed to the image of Christ. This, my friends, is not a three-dollar gospel.

FINDING LIFE BY CONNECTING TO JESUS

In this section we will consider the first movement of the Christ-centered life—finding life by connecting with Jesus. Of course this is foundational to the rest of what we will look at. To say that we find life by connecting with Jesus we will consider three aspects of what this looks like.

First, life is centered on building an ongoing conscious connection of our relationship with Jesus. This relationship, above all else, defines a believer. In chapters 2–4 we will look at practical ways of connecting to Jesus by focusing our attention on Him in how we view our past, how we live our present, and how we view our future.

Secondly, in chapter 5 we'll focus on how the Christ-centered life also flows from a growing dependency on the Holy Spirit. The Holy Spirit, the third person of the Trinitarian God, comes to make the believer alive to the reality of Jesus and to insure growing union with Him. To the degree that Christians either ignore the Holy Spirit or distort His role, union with Christ is compromised.

Finally, chapter 6 will show how the Christ-centered life must be submitted to the Word of God. To be absolutely clear, when I say "the Word" I am speaking of the Holy Bible. God has revealed His Word to His people in such a way that it is life and light to the soul. It is the healthy diet of the believer. To cease to feast on the Word is to cease to ingest Christ and thus to compromise our connection with Him.

And so we begin by looking at how we find life by connecting to Jesus.

2

DEVELOPING A LONGING TO KNOW JESUS

Christian people need no substitutes, no supplements, no boosters. Christ is all we need.

—Gardner C. Taylor

It does not take long to figure out what a person is passionate about. Our speech tells on us. Our actions betray us. To know a person well is to know what they love—what it is that really stirs their soul. You don't need the gift of discernment to figure out that one person is passionate about fishing, another loves art and a third is geeked out over computers. Our passions are obvious and they tell others something important about us.

The interesting thing about passions, however, is that many of them are not inbred at all but they are learned and cultivated. I enjoy sports. I grew up in a home with three boys and a father who played and watched sports. If there was a ball to be hit, kicked or thrown we wanted a piece of it. And so I began a love affair with baseball, football and basketball. As a child most of my free time involved sports in one way or another. Whether playing basketball for hours until it was too dark to play, or collecting cards or watching games on television, the focus was consistently on sports. Growing in a passion for sports was natural for me because it was encouraged by family and friends and met a deep need for me in finding my identity. To this day I have a great love for sports and get great enjoyment out of both competing and watching others compete. Cultivated passions are hard to kick.

FROM PASSION TO IDENTITY

Most of our passions grow in similar ways. Somehow a connection is triggered between something outside of us and something inside of us. For one person the inbred desire to be affirmed and loved is matched with an ability to make others laugh and they become the class clown. For another their ability in music, sports, or academics may be the thing that gains approval from their parents. At some point, through repetition, modeling and reinforcement we begin to grow in a passion and find that at least a part of our identity becomes attached to our involvement or performance in that activity.

The novel *Seven Days in Utopia*, by David Cook[1], describes a golfer whose whole identity became attached to his performance on the golf course. If he had a good day, he was a success or moving toward success. But if he had a bad day, he was a failure and a mess and nothing else mattered. Regardless of the specifics, we can all relate to finding our identity in unhealthy ways in passions that begin to rule over us.

As our identity becomes attached to our passions for the things of this world, we are set up for the ultimate failure. The irony of this is that when we succeed the most, and therefore feel the most alive, we are actually the farthest away from life. Of course this is not to say that there is anything wrong with succeeding at something—we should always be striving to do well. However, if our passion is not held in proper relation and connection to Christ, success often has the impact of driving us away from Him. Passions not rooted in relationship with Christ quickly become idols.

I vividly remember getting my first job when I graduated from college. I was accepted at a Fortune 500 company in the US headquarters of their marketing department. Buying my new suits, shirts and ties, I really thought I had arrived. As good as this was in many ways, it also came with a downside. I became a more arrogant person than I already was. Worse, because I was also a new believer I could not see my arrogance at all. My burgeoning pride masked itself as being a "man of faith." However, it was more like "look at me" faith than it was "thank the Lord" faith. Our sense of need for Jesus is easily dulled by the intoxication of those things that can never bring life. This is why success and riches in this world can so easily lead us away from sincere devotion to Christ.

DEVELOPING A PASSION FOR JESUS

So our question becomes: How do we develop a passion for Christ? David says in Psalm 27:4, "One thing have I asked of the Lord, that I will seek after: that I may dwell in the house of the Lord all the days of my life, to gaze upon the beauty of the Lord and to inquire in his temple." David's declaration is the result of a developed passion that holds out a singular affection. This is not just religious mumbo jumbo. By all appearances, what we see here in David is passion for God at a deep level.

The first three verses of this Psalm reveal much of what feeds this passion for David. In verse 1 he begins to sing the praises of God by His covenant name, "the Lord" or "Yahweh". He makes the statement, "The Lord is my light and salvation," and asks the rhetorical question, "Whom shall I fear?" He repeats and emphasizes this with the second half of the first verse that proclaims, "The Lord is the stronghold of my life," and then asks the question, "Of whom shall I be afraid?"

What is seen here is that the passion that David displays in verse 4 is fueled by his experience of God starting in verse 1. He has come to personally understand God as his "light," his "salvation" and as the "stronghold" of his life. Each of these metaphors is loaded with deep meaning for David. The first act of creation in Genesis 1 is the creation of light. In the Bible, light becomes a primary metaphor for the truth of God that is able to guide a believer (see Ps.43:3; 119:105; Prov. 6:23; Isa.2:5; 2 Pet.1:19). Ultimately, Jesus reveals Himself as the "light of the world" (see John 8:12; 9:5; 12:46; 1 John 1:5–7). David acknowledges that Yahweh is the one who brings him out of darkness and puts him on a right path. It has been the covenant faithfulness of God that has shown him the path of life over and over.

David says that the Lord is his "light and salvation." The Hebrew word for salvation is *yasha*. The word means to deliver, to rescue or to save.[2] In Exodus 14:13 Moses uses the word *yeshua* as he says to the people, "Fear not, stand firm and see the *salvation of the Lord* which he will work for you today. For the Egyptians whom you see today, you shall never see again." The Hebrew word for salvation in this verse is the word *yeshua* from which we get the Old Testament name "Joshua." In the New Testament this becomes the name Jesus, which means "the Lord saves." Standing by the Red Sea with Pharaoh's army coming to destroy them, Moses tells the people to stand by and see the *Yeshua Yahweh* or the "salvation of the Lord." David recalls the powerful saving work of the Lord in his life and, therefore, is able to proclaim with great confidence that he has no need for fear.

The Red Sea was a figure and type of that salvation which was ultimately won for us in the person and work of Yeshua/Jesus. Have you experienced the *Yeshua Yahweh*? The truth is that if you are willing to admit it, you also have many occurrences in your life where God has rescued, saved and delivered you. If you had no events in your life to look back on and see how the Lord has delivered you, you can still look back to Jesus' death on the cross as the definitive act of saving you from the wrath that you rightly deserve. The beginning of developing a passionate longing for God as you move forward in life is looking backwards to remember His faithfulness in delivering you in the past.

Lastly, we see the image of God as a "stronghold." According to the *African Bible Commentary*, "The image of God as a 'stronghold' is also a military one; for a stronghold was a place where one can be safe from all enemies. Because the Lord is his light, deliverer and refuge, the psalmist does not fear any threat. His rhetorical questions, *whom shall I fear?* and *of whom shall I be afraid?* are statements of faith."[3] Through the use of the images of light, salvation and stronghold, David is declaring that he is willing and able to put his full confidence in God as the one who will keep him. What other sources are you putting confidence in that are leading you away from a robust hope in God alone?

REMEMBERING WHAT GOD HAS DONE

Scripture continually emphasizes that God's people should remember His saving acts. In the Old Testament, the feast of the Passover was the continual reminder of how Yahweh delivered Israel from Egypt, Pharaoh, and the depths of the sea. In the New Testament the continual celebration of the Lord's Supper, or communion, is the perpetual reminder of the death of Christ for our sins. The Lord's supper also reminds believers that Jesus is coming back again for His children.

However, such a focus on grateful remembrance is swimming upstream against the tide of our fallen human nature and our culture. Ecclesiastes tell us that the eye is never satisfied with seeing and the ear is never satisfied with hearing (1:8). The natural disposition of human beings fallen in sin is to find reasons to be dissatisfied. We live in a culture where we are bombarded by messages that keep us from any meaningful experience of lasting satisfaction. The consistent message of advertising is that contentment can only be achieved with having what you do not have, and once you have it, it is outdated before you know it. Solomon might have told us, "consider your iPhone."

Whether it's Apples or Androids, the message being marketed is simple—you need the next best thing. And that thing—flatter, lighter, bigger (or smaller), awesomely "apped up" with new functions that will blow your mind—is outdated in six months! Like the gerbil on the treadmill, we run hard for it but we are getting nowhere.

Years ago I worked with a boy named "Jimmy" who lived in a section of North Philadelphia referred to as the Badlands. Jimmy lived with his mother and sisters, and the family would move every few months because they would get evicted for not paying rent. Jimmy was a great kid and I enjoyed my time working with him. I soon noticed however that Jimmy always had a new pair of expensive Air Jordan sneakers. It seemed that a month would not go by that he did not get a new pair of expensive sneakers. He would make fun of my "bobo" sneakers all the time, and we would both laugh at my unfashionable footwear. In my mind I could never understand how he could afford such sneakers.

One day I saw a pair of Air Jordans on sale at a sneaker store for ten dollars. I bought them right away and couldn't wait for Jimmy to see them. When I finally saw him he laughed at me harder than ever. Even though the sneakers were brand new and were genuine, he laughed because the model was over a year old. What had sold for one hundred dollars a year earlier was now worth only ten dollars not because it cost less to produce or had any less intrinsic value as a shoe, but because the new model made it obsolete. I soon found out that even my Air Jordans were bobos!

Western economics are built on creating an artificial need in the consumer that eats away at any possibility of contentment. Whether it is Jimmy buying sneakers he could not afford or any of us making sure we get the "next big thing" in technology, we are bombarded with the message that we need something more.

Contrast this message with God's call to grateful contentment. "Godliness with contentment is great gain" writes Paul (1 Tim. 6:6). Contentment is established by consistently remembering the work of Christ on your behalf. In the course of a day there are scores of situations, circumstances and occurrences that will cause you to forget, neglect, undervalue or doubt the finished work of Jesus for you. Some crisis makes us wonder if God still cares about us. Some successes leave us drunk with ourselves and neglecting what is of utmost importance. Some temptations lead us to look for life where it can never be found and forget the source of true life that we have in Jesus.

THE HABIT OF REMEMBERING GOD

You will only increase your longing for Christ if you consciously develop a habitual lifestyle of remembering what He has done for you. Once a week at church won't cut it. Once a day in a devotional time is better but is still woefully insufficient. Developing a habit of remembering God's faithfulness throughout the day is necessary. You will not long for what you do not cherish. You will not cherish that which you easily forget. Like David, we must use our minds to focus on God's faithfulness that is manifested most perfectly in Jesus Christ. Making Jesus the object of constant remembrance is the only remedy to bring us real transformation.

In Psalm 84:10 the psalmist says, "For a day in your courts is better than a thousand elsewhere. I would rather be a doorkeeper in the house of my God than dwell in the tents of wickedness." These words betray a deep passion for God. Like David, the psalmist here indicates a fervent desire to be close to God. This is the heart of true worship. Two primary analogies are used which indicate an obsessive longing to be with God.

The first contrast is that of time. The psalmist prefers one day with his Lord to a thousand anywhere else. Are you catching the significance of this? A day is here and gone. It is easily forgotten. In a moment, with the next turn of events in life, yesterday fades quickly from memory. Today's crisis or triumphs, tomorrow's looming disasters or anticipated victories, relegate yesterday into a place of little or no import. But not so with the psalmist! He understands significance not by the length of time but by relationship and proximity. One day in close proximity to God is worth more than a hundred lifetimes spent out of his presence. In forceful poetic language he is saying that life apart from God is not really life at all. All life derives its significance from relationship to God and proximity to Him. Even if that proximity is fleeting, one day in God's courts is enough to sustain him for a lifetime.

Secondly he contrasts degrees of intimacy. "I would rather be a doorkeeper in the house of my God than dwell in the tents of wickedness." It is hard to think of a position with less intimacy than that of a doorkeeper. He stays on the fringes, on the outskirts of what is really going on. Contrast that to one who "dwells" or lives in the lavish tents of the prosperous. The dweller is on the inside—where the action is. He gets to experience everything that his host experiences. Nothing is held back from him because he is within the inner circle. And yet the psalmist finds the position of the doorkeeper to be the preferred place. Why?

The key for the psalmist is not having a position of privileged relationship but having relationship with true privilege. He considers relationship with his God a privilege beyond any other. The Hebrew word which is translated as "doorkeeper" is used only here in the Old Testament. The NET Bible makes this note about the usage of this word: "Traditionally some have interpreted this as a reference to being a doorkeeper at the temple, though some understand it to mean "lie as a beggar at the entrance to the temple.[4] The contrast here is significant. The psalmist prefers the position of a beggar with close proximity to God over a position of privilege in the tents of the wicked without God. His taste buds for the world's lavish goods have been ruined. His longing is to be close to the only one who holds all of life in his hands.

A key to understanding his passion is the psalmist's first person possessive relationship with God. He is not just excited about being a doorkeeper in the house of God, but in the house of "*my God*." He knows God. He loves God. His worth and value is derived from relationship with God and God alone. He is content to have his God determine where and how he will serve. He just wants to serve Him. Though he may not be in the back room with the prophets, priests and kings, he is satisfied. He is "in the building" and serving his God.

I want my walk with God to be like that. To be honest it often is not. I struggle with my personal insecurities and with entitlement that comes from thinking more of myself than I should. But I am reminded over and over that my primary blessing comes not from what I accomplish but from whose team I am on. God is at work remaking me to value my relationship with Him above my accomplishments. Does this ring true in your life? Are you seeing more clearly that the things that you once thought you needed for real satisfaction can never produce what they promise?

ENTITLEMENT, DISILLUSIONMENT OR GRATITUDE?

There are two primary competitors to a life that is marked by thankfulness and gratitude. Entitlement is the disposition that takes for granted that you are owed some special privileges or blessings just because of who you are. These privileges are almost always focused on things that will make my life more comfortable, more pleasurable, or increase my sense of self-worth in the eyes of myself and others. Entitlement is the strong curse of western twenty-first-century culture. At the root of entitlement is the lie of Satan to Eve in Genesis 3 that says "you will be like God." The effect of living in a constant state of entitlement, is that we functionally live as if the world should be geared to give us what we desire. The entitled cannot be pleased.

One sure sign of an entitlement ethos is a strong proclivity to boredom. The entitled will not be thankful. The entitled will not be satisfied. Ultimately for those who refuse to come off the high horse of entitlement, disillusionment is the inevitable result.

Disillusionment is the condition in which our eyes are opened to see things and people as they actually are. Disillusionment bursts the bubble of entitlement and often leads to cynicism and depression[5]. Having discovered that life does not revolve around me (although I still think it should), I am prone to anger, sadness and resignation at the "unfairness" of life. When we neglect to grow in a disposition of gratitude, we inevitably cycle between entitlement and cynical disillusionment. This cycle leads us far away from intimacy with God and negatively impacts every other earthly relationship as well. Growing in gratitude, contentment and thankfulness towards God is a critical foundation in the upward movement to establish real intimacy with God and realize on a consistent basis that Jesus is the center of our lives.

What are you doing to develop a greater and more consistent passion for God in your life? This is not the same as asking about how you are doing in overcoming some specific area of sin. Based on what has already been discussed in this chapter let me suggest a specific way to move towards God by growing in gratitude for God in your life.

THE DISCIPLINE OF THANKFULNESS

In order to develop a greater passion for Jesus in our lives, believers must develop a habitual lifestyle of thanksgiving for what God has done. As believers we must consistently reflect with thanksgiving on the faithfulness of God in our lives. This is not to be confused with a time of Bible reading, Bible study or general prayer but it can include those elements. These are specific times where you verbally recall with thanksgiving how God has been faithful to you. It is a time to recount with thanksgiving the truth of the gospel—Jesus Christ has died for my sins, Jesus has risen from the grave, Jesus sits at the right hand of the Father interceding for me. It is a time to remember the blessings He has given you both in the past and up to the present day. This can be done at the beginning of a time of prayer as a primary element of prayer. Paul admonishes the Philippians to "not be anxious about anything, but in everything by prayer and supplication *with thanksgiving* let your requests be made known to God" (Phil. 4:6).

When circumstances are very difficult in life the discipline of thankfulness may seem impossible to maintain. Poverty, tragedy, pain and suffering introduce both difficult challenges and important opportunities to experience God in a new way. Paul speaks of this experience as he writes these words to the Corinthian church:

> So we do not lose heart. Though our outer self is wasting away, our inner self is being renewed day by day. For this light momentary affliction is preparing for us an eternal weight of glory beyond all comparison, as we look not to the things that are seen but to the things

> that are unseen. For the things that are seen are transient, but the things that are unseen are eternal. (2 Cor. 4:16–18)

These remarkable verses demonstrate a perspective on suffering by Paul that is commended to all those who follow Christ. What Paul calls "light momentary affliction" includes repeatedly being thrown in jail, beaten, stoned and left for dead, being betrayed and forsaken by those close to him and fulfilling his ministry as a single man never taking a wife. With all of these things, however, he has an eternal perspective that values the inner man more than the outer man and the things that are unseen more than the things that are seen. He glories in the fact that through all of these things he and those whom he ministers to are being prepared for "an eternal weight of glory beyond all comparison." The key to growing in the discipline of thankfulness and therefore contentment is developing an eternal perspective that values what is nearest to the heart of God far above that which makes life pleasant in the moment.

DEVELOPING THE DISCIPLINE OF THANKFULNESS

Let me offer a few suggestions that I have found helpful in developing the discipline of thankfulness. 1) Be consistent in voicing your thankfulness to God at least three times a day—morning, midday and evening. 2) At every opportunity remember the cross and the love of God for you, demonstrated by Jesus as He died to pay the penalty for your sins. 3) Give thanks for your present circumstances. If you need to ask God for perspective to do this then ask Him. It is important that you see, acknowledge and give thanks for how God is presently at work in our life.[6]

Thankfulness is a foundational character quality for a growing Christian. Although thankfulness is developed as a discipline, it soon becomes much more than that. A thankful heart is the good soil that readily receives God's word. Hurting people, and those who are struggling can easily connect with a grateful person because their gratefulness is a repudiation of pride and arrogance. The thankful person is not under the illusion that they have "pulled themselves up by their bootstraps." Instead they are grateful knowing that although they did not deserve to be pulled up, God in His infinite mercy, has chosen to lovingly act on their behalf. As I grow in thankfulness my accomplishments appear smaller and God's grace looms larger.

Isn't it a blessing to be around thankful people? Contrast that with keeping company with people who are always complaining. Now I know that at many times in my life I have been that complaining person. The thankful person adds life and joy to others. The complaining person takes life and joy from others. The interesting thing is that the difference between the two is not their circumstances but their disposition. Will you choose to live in a disposition of thankfulness?

I don't want to suggest that developing the discipline of thankfulness is a simple as one, two, three. It is not. That is why it is a discipline! This is absolutely critical, though, if you will draw near to God. No healthy person draws near to someone that they believe is out to hurt them. When we rehearse God's faithfulness we prepare the soil of our hearts to receive Jesus.

To cultivate the upward movement that reorients our life toward God we move from entitlement and disillusionment to gratitude and thankfulness. As you develop the discipline of thankfulness it will become more and more natural to desire to prioritize spending more time with God. Your consistent acknowledgement of God's steadfast love towards you leads you to desire His presence and to draw near to Him.

O Lord our God,
Help us to desire You above all things,
To long for Your presence more than our comfort,
To yearn to know You above being known by others,
To put away our pride that we may put on
Your righteousness.
Create in us clean hearts,
And renew a right spirit within us,
That You alone might receive glory from our lives.
We ask this through our Lord Jesus Christ, Your Son,
Who lives and reigns with You
and the Holy Spirit,
One God, forever and ever. Amen.

3

STOPPING TO BE WITH JESUS

God can't give us peace and happiness apart from Himself because there is no such thing.

—C.S. Lewis

As a young boy I did not like reading. I mean really, give me the choice between running around, throwing a ball or playing anything and sitting down to read a book? Are you kidding? For me as a ten-year-old boy I did not need to ponder this for long. Reading meant sitting still when my body wanted to run around. Reading meant letting my toys just sit there when I knew they were longing to be played with. Playing won over reading every time. For my ten-year-old self this was the ultimate no brainer!

But over time something began to change. I remember looking forward to getting the Sunday newspaper and reading the sports page. Back in the days before the Internet and ESPN the Sunday paper was my lifeline to the world of sports that I loved so much. I would pour over the statistics of my favorite players and find out not just what the score was but also learn about what was happening behind the scenes. A new world started to open up for me. I actually enjoyed reading because I was getting something out of it that I liked. Soon I began reading books about my favorite sports heroes and then one day I ventured into strange waters. I picked up a *Hardy Boys* novel that my older brother had—and I enjoyed it. I was now actually enjoying reading and beginning a journey that has blessed my life immeasurably. Like a drug addict, I started with the soft stuff and gradually worked my way up to the hard stuff. Over a long period of time my love for reading and learning grew into a greater and greater passion.

Developing a longing for Christ takes time and effort. I once heard it said that developing bad habits is easy and breaking them is exceedingly difficult. I'm not sure if this is true. I have broken my bad habit of biting my nails hundreds of times! Conversely, developing good habits is difficult and breaking them is extraordinarily easy. To be honest I have found this to be true on both counts and this helps us to understand why developing a consistent longing for Christ, one that makes our infatuation with this world grow dim, is so difficult. Like a little boy who just wants to run around a play, our flesh does not want to slow down to be with Jesus when there is so much more "fun stuff" to do.

LIVING WITH BROKENNESS

We are broken people. People who do not know Jesus Christ as Lord are broken. People who do know Jesus Christ as Lord are broken. Baptists, Catholics, Presbyterians, Methodists and Pentecostals are broken. Atheists, agnostics, Buddhists, Hindus, Muslims and Mormons are broken. Whether ministers or mechanics, priests or prostitutes, pastors or pole dancers, we are all broken. Our brokenness transcends race, class and gender. It transcends labels such as conservative or liberal, right-wing or left-wing, urban or rural, majority or minority. The fall of humankind into sin, detailed in Genesis chapter three, has left us broken and in need of healing, restoration and salvation. The need is desperate and the need is universal.

Quoting Jeremiah, Paul writes these words in Romans 3:10-12:

> "None is righteous, no, not one;
> no one understands;
> no one seeks for God.
> All have turned aside; together they have become worthless;
> no one does good,
> not even one."

In this passage, Paul is pointing out that everyone is enslaved by sin. For a first-century Jew like Paul, the world was divided into two groups—Jews and Gentiles. Paul says that there is no distinction between these groups in terms of their need for God. There are no exceptions "not even one." This was a radical idea that Paul was introducing. For the first-century Jew there was a clear delineation of worth and value for Jews and Gentiles. The Jew was of the chosen people. They considered Gentiles as dogs, subhuman, worthless. For Paul to level the playing field (as Jesus had done before him) was an unspeakable indignity. How dare he!

How is your world divided? Christians and non-Christians? Republicans and Democrats? Heterosexuals and homosexuals? Whatever, wherever and however you divide, your groups, just like Paul's, have the same common, basic need. They are broken sinners who seek their own comfort ahead of seeking God.

Does it strike you as strange that I lumped Christians and non-Christians in the same pot? This is a reality check. In terms of our present brokenness we are in many ways more alike than different. If this is true then what difference does it make to be a believer in Christ? The truth is that it makes all the difference in the world and then some. For Jesus Christ alone is the remedy for our lost condition. Although believers remain broken they are now in the process of receiving the healing that they need. Although they still suffer in brokenness they are now beginning to see some of the fractures coming together. Christians/Christ-followers now live with the sure promises of God. In the book of Revelation the apostle John puts the promise in these words:

> Therefore they are before the throne of God,
> and serve him day and night in his temple;
> and he who sits on the throne will shelter them with his presence.
> They shall hunger no more, neither thirst anymore;
> the sun shall not strike them,
> nor any scorching heat.
> For the Lamb in the midst of the throne will be their shepherd,
> and he will guide them to springs of living water,
> and God will wipe away every tear from their eyes.
> (Rev. 7:15-17)

This promise is one of many that speaks of the blessedness that is the inheritance of those who live for Christ. The promise is given in the context of the fierce struggle that Jesus followers experience living in a fallen world and in unredeemed bodies. When we realize the degree and depth of our brokenness then we understand that nothing less than radical dependence upon God is sufficient.

MODERN DAY PHARISEES

In these days many people see "radical Islam" as the greatest threat to the Christian church. Actually, I am more afraid of the threat that comes from "good Christians." Like Jesus' first-century opponents, the Pharisees, "good Christians" emphasize their superiority to others in a multitude of ways. They emphasize areas where their outward compliance to a standard is commendable. They may have truly overcome some life-debilitating areas of sin that now make them acceptable, presentable and even enviable to others. The problem is, just like the Pharisees, they deny the obvious rottenness that is still fastidiously attached to them.

Jesus said that the Pharisees were like whitewashed tombstones. They looked really nice on the outside, but on the inside they were "full of dead people's bones and all unclenness" (Matt. 23:27). Outward compliance to certain standards and some nonessential doctrines that are now seen as essential becomes the measuring stick of "true believers." When this happens the gospel of Jesus Christ is effectively jettisoned as the means of salvation and replaced with modern day pharisaic legalism. This is truly the greatest threat to the gospel in our day.

Desperate dependence on Christ is not promoted by faith in my moral progress. If I get really honest, my moral progress is really quite negligible. I can only count any progress as the grace of God at work in my life. In fact the closer I get to Christ the more I am aware of my filthiness and the less I have to boast in. *The more intense the light, the clearer every blemish becomes.* Developing a track record of resisting temptation is a blessing of God's grace. Knowing that if God's grace was taken away for even a moment I would quickly find myself in a deeper cesspool of moral filth than I could ever imagine keeps me desperate for God. This knowledge is not just a theoretical "what if" that is used as some kind of straw man argument. This is something I live with daily. I am reminded continually of my own evil inclinations and my ability to make decisions that temporarily dismiss God in order to indulge in ungodly passions.

Perhaps this is why near the end of his life Paul calls himself the "worst" of all sinners (1 Tim. 1:15). He also calls himself "unworthy to be called an apostle" (1 Cor. 15:9) and "the very least of the saints" (Eph. 3:8). This does not sound like a man who is full of himself but one who boasts in Christ alone.

THE CALL TO ABIDE

The chief admonition of Jesus to His disciples as He was about to be crucified was that they abide in Him. "Abide in me, and I in you," Jesus says (John 15:4). He goes on to say, "as the branch cannot bear fruit by itself, unless it abides in the vine, neither can you, unless you abide in me." The word translated "abide" is the Greek word *meno*. This word means to reside somewhere, to live somewhere or to stay somewhere[1]. It emphasizes continuity, permanence and stability. Jesus admonishes His disciples to dwell with Him and not to go anywhere else. The only possibility they have of a life that is actually fruitful is that they stay directly and permanently connected to Him. A branch disconnected from a vine does not have within it what it takes to produce fruit. The vine is connected to the roots which take in the water and nutrients from the soil which are able to produce fruit.

This then becomes the metaphor that accurately describes the position of every person who says that they believe in Christ. A confession of Christ is a good start, but Jesus cautions that if we do not stay connected to Him with permanence and stability our lives will not produce fruit. He warns that "if anyone does not abide in me he is thrown away like a branch and withers; and the branches are gathered, thrown into the fire, and burned" (John 15:6).

This makes clear that the great challenge of the Christian life is staying consciously and viably connected to Jesus at all times. A disconnected branch ceases to function as a branch at all. In Jesus' words such branches are gathered together and thrown into the fire to be burned. This is nothing less than a picture of eternal separation from God in hell.

Jesus' disciples would have easily connected this word picture with the place just outside of Jerusalem where all the refuse of the city was burned—Gehenna. This place was known in Hebrew as the Valley of Hinnom (transliterated into Greek as Gehenna). It had been used by idolatrous Jews to offer of their children as sacrifices to the false god Molech during the Israelite monarchy. "This valley afterwards became the common receptacle for all the refuse of the city. Here the dead bodies of animals and of criminals, and all kinds of filth, were cast and consumed by fire kept always burning. It thus in process of time became the image of the place of everlasting destruction."[2] This word, "Gehenna," was used by Jesus to refer to the place of everlasting punishment and is translated in English Bibles as "hell" (Matt. 5:22, 29, 30; 10:28; 18:9; 23:15, 33; Mark 9:43, 45, 47; Luke 12:5; James 3:6).

Clearly in speaking these words to His disciples, Jesus has in mind Judas, who has already left to betray him and will eventually commit suicide. Judas is about to become the living embodiment of these words. Disconnected from Jesus by his own pride, greed and idolatry he sinks to the lowest abyss of the human condition. Jesus did not disconnect Judas from Himself—Judas did. The act of eternal separation is not God imposing His will against people who desire to be connected to Him. This separation is instead God's willingness to give to them what they have stubbornly asked for in spite of His pleas to the contrary.

The tragic reality is that the separation from God that Judas experienced is experienced by many who likewise choose other things over Jesus. Sadly, I have known several people who by every indication seemed to love Jesus and wanted to live for Him, but for one reason or another walked away from Christ and Christianity. Many fall for the gospel of positive self-affirmation that does away with personal sin and guilt. The issue is that it also reduces Jesus to nothing more than a good moral example. He ceases to be the sin-bearing Savior that we actually need. For those who adopt this ideology, the mad rush to distance themselves from sin and guilt is what actually leaves them standing guilty before a holy God. For others the relentless call to materialism or the unwillingness to give up the pleasures of sin cause them to fall back from following Jesus. In every tragic instance they are choosing to be connected to something other than Jesus.

For this reason we must pay especially close attention to our inner life which we will look at in more detail later. For now it is enough to say that abiding in Christ must never become simply an emotional high that is experienced or an abstract intellectual phenomenon. Abiding happens in the daily, hourly, and minute-by-minute decisions that are guided by a growing and true knowledge of Jesus. He is the True Vine. Finding life in any other vine will eventually lead to death.

THE GOD OF PURPOSE

I remember my son playing soccer when he was a young child. If you have ever had the blessing of watching youth soccer you know that in spite of expert coaching you have a group of about ten children running around in a scrum after the ball at any given time. It is a hilarious sight. Well my son, Joshua, just happened to be a little faster and a little bit more skilled than the other kids. Because of this, when he got the ball he would generally score. He would score anywhere from five to eight goals in a game. I remember one of the other parents coming to me very concerned because he did not pass the ball enough. I understood what he was saying but I thought, "Gosh, isn't the purpose of the game to score?"

God has created everything for a purpose. The sun gives light and warmth. In addition to giving us light in the night by reflecting the sun, the moon plays an important role in controlling the tides. The heart pumps our blood, the lungs bring in air and I'm sure the pancreas does something too! The idea is that God is a purposeful creator and that you and I are a part of His grand tapestry of creation. We were created to image Him in the world. Like the moon, however, we have no light in and of ourselves. The light that we shine is derived light—it is not intrinsic to us, but is the property of God Himself. Because of this, fulfilling our purpose in life is totally contingent upon one thing—living in close proximity to the True Light, or put another way, abiding in Jesus Christ.

THE NECESSITY OF PRUNING

Let's look a little closer at what Jesus says to His disciples in John 15. In verse 1 He gives them the analogy that He is the True Vine and His father is the Vinedresser. In verse 2 He lets them know that every vine that does not produce fruit is "taken away" and every branch that does produce fruit is "pruned." In verse 6, which we have looked at above, He explicitly tells us that unproductive branches will be cut off and thrown into the fire. It is interesting that according to Jesus' words every branch is going to get cut one way or another.

Pruning occurs in the life of those who produce fruit in order that they will produce a greater quantity of fruit in the future. The vinedresser knows that he must prune all but the most vibrant shoots in order to produce vibrant branches that are securely attached to the vine. These branches are then able to produce a plentiful harvest because all of the nonessential growth, which would have otherwise taken up precious water and nutrients, has be cut away.

So it is with believers. God is always in the process of pruning from us those things that hinder our ability to produce fruit for Christ. There is no special quality of the branch other than that it is attached to vine. It is not the value of the container (the branch) but the value of what is contained. Christ flowing into the life of the believer is what distinguishes him or her from others. And if Christ flows through my life there will be genuine fruit that validates this truth.

The "connection" of those who do not produce fruit is really no connection at all. In agriculture dead branches can occur for several different reasons. Most commonly a branch dies because of insufficient light, pests and disease damage. Because of these factors the life-giving sap that comes from the tree itself can no longer be found in the dead branch. If the dead branch remains connected to the tree there is a high likelihood that it will affect the whole tree. Therefore the only solution is to cut off the dead branch to preserve the integrity of the tree.

Pruning is the process of cutting off what is dead in order to bring greater life and vitality to what is yet alive. Jesus is clear that every person has "dead places" that need pruning in order to produce greater fruit in their lives. Dead places are any area of your life where you know you are not putting Jesus first. Spending huge amounts of unproductive time on video games, television or surfing the web can be a dead place. Having deep relationships with unbelievers that cause us to compromise our convictions can be a dead place. The desire for material things that causes us to be stingy in our giving can be a dead place.

Jesus is telling believing disciples that He is coming after the dead places with His pruning shears. This is not a warning but a welcomed promise to every believer who wants their life to count for Jesus. Pruning is welcomed by the healthy branch because it will allow that branch to be more productive. It allows the branch to more fully realize its potential to accomplish what it was created for.

My experience of life in Christ is that God is the perfect gardener. Although my laziness or inattention may lead me to neglect pruning, God is neither lazy nor forgetful. There is never much time that goes by before God once again pulls out His pruning shears. Most often this can take the form of trials and difficulties in my life that serve to let me know that I may not be as far along in my relationship with God as I thought. Like the disciples on the sea with Jesus in Luke chapter 8, when the storm gets really bad I may find that my faith is not where I thought it was. In His pruning grace God has consistently shown me where I am not in order to grow me to be more like Him.

THE FRUIT OF ABIDING

For the believer, pruning is getting rid of everything in life that does not produce fruit for Christ. Jesus gives a very simple and yet profound prescription for disciples to produce greater levels of fruitfulness in their lives—abiding in Him! Jesus uses a form of the word "abide" eight times in John 15 between verses 4 and 10. He is saying in the clearest possible way with repeated emphasis that the primary lifestyle emphasis of believers is to ensure that they stay vitally connected to Jesus at all times. Abiding in Christ is the key to:

1. Bearing fruit for Christ, even "much fruit" (John 14:4, 5, 8)
2. Possessing the ability to do anything that pleases God (14:5)
3. Knowing the security of God's love (14:6)
4. An effective prayer life (14:7)
5. Experiencing God's lavish love (14:9, 10)
6. 6. Keeping God's commandments (14:10)
7. Experiencing the fullness of joy that is available through Christ (14:11)

Understanding this, it becomes clear that abiding in Christ is the primary challenge and the most necessary reality that defines the life of a believer. Outside of this ongoing connection there is no credible evidence that a person is a believer at all! Jesus warns His disciples that the way that they can recognize false prophets is by their fruit (see Matt. 7:15-20). Ultimately, Jesus says, "every tree that does not bear good fruit is cut down and thrown into the fire (7:19). In John 14:15 Jesus says, "If you love me you will keep my commandments." It is clear that only by abiding in Christ will a believer live a fruitful life where there is a growing desire to honor Jesus through obedience.

How then can believers stay vitally connected to Jesus in a world that mitigates against this ongoing connection in every imaginable way? The Scripture outlines two critical elements to keeping this connection with these words, "work out your own salvation with fear and trembling, for it is God who works in you, both to will and to work for his good pleasure" (Phil. 2:12–13).

THE WAY OF ABIDING

First of all, we stay connected by ongoing conscious effort and discipline. It is very important to remember that the "reset" button on our flesh is our own comfort and ease (especially as it pertains to the things of God). Without disciplined effort we will quickly "fall off the bandwagon." This is true for the newest believer or the most seasoned saint. "Work out your own salvation with fear and trembling," Paul says to the Philippians (2:12). Scripture is clearly letting us know that it is our responsibility to continually work to maintain our conscious connection with Christ through our ongoing effort.

I am afraid that too often in modern evangelicalism we have made the mistake of calling discipline legalism. This is a profoundly debilitating lie of the Enemy. Legalism is the attempt to justify ourselves by our works. Healthy discipline for the believer is the attempt to live in a way that glorifies God. I know that I have fallen for this lie at times myself and used it as an excuse not to embrace God by not honoring discipline and practices that would enable me to grow closer to Jesus. Effort, work, and discipline must not become dirty words in the Christian vocabulary. In a fallen world, living for Christ will mean embracing hard work and discipline in order to live a life that brings great glory to God.

Secondly, we stay connected by acknowledging that even the desire we have to stay connected to Christ is a gift from God. The reason that Christians should work out their salvation with fear and trembling is that "it is God who works in you, both to will and to work for his good pleasure" (Phil. 2:13). This is critical to a healthy foundation in Christian discipleship. The Lord makes clear that both the desire to please Him (our will) and the ability to follow through on that desire (our work) is a gift from God.

Our "work" in centering our lives on a relationship with Jesus is empowered by God himself, but it is still our work! This is not something for clergy, clerics and monks but for every believer. The lifestyle of the believer must be marked by stopping to be with God often. This must become a part of the daily, weekly, monthly and yearly lifestyle of the believer if they are to progress in holiness and fruitful Christian living.

This is a radical call on the lives of Christians. If Christ has suffered the full weight of the penalty of our sins (and He has), and has overcome death, hell and the grave for us (and He has), why are we so caught up in trivial realities that keep our lives anesthetized from the true drama of life! We are not here to make a few bucks and brag about how well our kids are doing! We exist as players engaged in the saga to end all sagas. On a scale so grand that angels look on in awe, we are integral parts of the ongoing redeeming work of Christ that makes war against all demonic forces that attempt to practically nullify the work of the cross. This is not science fiction—this is real life.

I know that I have often fallen into this demonic amnesia. The pressures of life with difficult relationships, cars that don't work, computers that crash and more month than money have led me to focus so closely on what is right in my face that I miss the bigger picture. It is only as I come to Jesus and remember the centrality of my calling to be with Him that I am able to put all the other stuff into perspective and remember why I am here in the first place.

I remember being in seminary in 1990. I had my first personal computer, a Macintosh, and I was thrilled to be writing my first paper on biblical exegesis. I was thrilled until, on page 20 of the paper, my screen went black and a small bomb appeared in the middle of it! To me that bomb now meant everything. All I had been learning about the gospel of John was gone from my head. My wife and children no longer seemed to matter. My job, my church, my money . . . nothing mattered anymore but the little bomb in the middle of the screen. For me that little bomb almost made me forget my salvation! That little bomb became my reality.

It is interesting how adversity can reveal the sad reality of just how selfish we are. I totally lost perspective on my life and God's purpose for me because I encountered a setback. This is exactly why centering our lives on Jesus is so important. If we are not rightly centered we quickly forget who we are and why we are here.

As Jesus instructs His disciples regarding prayer, He comforts them with these words: "Ask and you shall receive, seek and you shall find, knock and the door shall be opened to you" (Matt. 7:7). While these certainly are comforting words, they are also much more than that. Each of the verbs in the sentence is in the imperative mood in Greek.[3] This is the mood of command. This means that Jesus is not just suggesting prayer as a good idea but He is commanding it. Furthermore each of the verbs is in the Greek present tense which signifies ongoing continuing action.[4] In other words the force of the statement is "ask and *keep on asking*, seek and *keep on seeking*, knock and *keep on knocking*." This is not occasionally throwing up a prayer to the "man upstairs" but an ongoing perpetual bombardment of the throne of heaven by those who follow Jesus Christ.

CHALLENGING THE RHYTHM OF LIFE

If we are to make Christ central to our lives then the rhythms of our lives need to center on Him. Jesus Christ replaces anything and everything that would demand our allegiance in such a way as to make Him anything less than the supreme ruler and object of our affections.

What might this look like practically in your life? Of course this will mean that how you spend your time must change. Beyond just changing your schedule, however, it means first and foremost a reestablishing of priorities based on the supremacy of Christ. Unless your heart is changed to desire Christ above all, your schedule change will not last long!

Practically, this will mean making more time for Jesus in your life. You will never "find" this time but you must aggressively make it. Pressing into Christ, which is the call for every Christian, is never comfortable or easy. It will mean cutting out some things that are good or pleasurable, in order to focus on what is best.

I remember picking up one of my daughters from her day care when she was three years old. She repeated a saying that she had just learned. "Good better best, I'll never take a rest, until my good is better and my better is my best!" I'm sure she had no clue about what this meant, but it was certainly precious to hear these words from the lips of my little one. How do you suppose God would hear those words coming from your lips? With a heart truly desiring to make the best use of time in order to connect often with Jesus, this will change your daily patterns.

This kind of change will involve your devotional life of prayer, Scripture reading and meditation and your community life. In the midst of the busyness of life will you stop to be with Jesus often and build in daily and weekly routines that demonstrate that He really is prized above all other things? This will not be sustainable if it is merely fueled by a legalistic zeal to check this off of your "good Christian" checklist. In fact that zeal will run out sooner rather than later.

PURSUING HARD AFTER GOD

The fuel for this discipline is a growing love for God and dependence upon the Holy Spirit. For now it is enough to say that practically putting Jesus Christ in the position of supremacy in your life will mean replacing a comfortable or casual approach to your relationship with God to resemble one that looks like aggressively pursuing a relationship with someone who has fully captured your heart. The young lover pursues hard after the beloved. Indeed, whether you know it or not, this is how God is pursing you.

Just making up your mind to read more, pray more, or be involved in more "church activities" is not the answer. There is a fundamental change at the heart level that God is after. Several practices that I have embraced have been of great benefit for me in this. One is stopping many times a day to say a short prayer which helps me to set my mind on Jesus. The prayer that I use is an ancient prayer called the "Jesus Prayer" which I have made some additions to. This has helped me to form a greater awareness of Jesus throughout my day. I usually say this slowly and reflectively before I get out of bed in the morning and at various points throughout the day. In Appendix 1 of this book I explain more about the history of this prayer and how I have used it as a part of my own spiritual formation.

Another practice that I have embraced is that of the daily office (also known as the Divine Hours or the Work of God). I was introduced to this by Peter Scazzero in his life changing book, *Emotionally Healthy Spirituality.*[5] Drawing on the practice of monastics, this is a radical change to the idea of "doing devotions" that is so much a part of evangelical practice. While devotions are usually looked at as something that is done once a day, the practice of daily office recognizes our need to connect with God several times a day. Saint Benedict prescribed stopping eight times a day for the divine office over which nothing else was to be preferred. His rule was set for the monks who lived in the monastery and has been followed by many for the last 1,500 years.[6] While eight times a day may be way too much for those of us living on the outside of the monastery, the idea that we must stop several times a day is critical. Through a combination of prayer, Scripture reading, meditation and silence, the idea of the daily office is not so much to get something from God as to be with God.[7] During a workday this can be as simple as taking a ten-minute break to re-center your life on Jesus. This has become an invaluable practice in my life over the last several years. For more information on this, I highly recommend reading *Emotionally Healthy Spirituality* by Peter Scazerro.

Let me ask you a question. What would be different in your life if you lived as if success in every area depended totally on Jesus Christ? The specific answers to what you need to do with your time and schedule are wrapped up in answering that question honestly and wisely. Deep reflection on this and the engagement of wise counselors who have embraced a deeper walk with Jesus are critical.

TAKING THE NEXT STEP

Perhaps the most critical outward change to help most of us live more fully for Jesus is in the area of relationships. You will not become a person who walks in deep communion with God if you do not have significant relationships with others who are doing the same thing. Essentially, who you are and what you care about is revealed primarily by whom you spend time with and how you spend time with them. As you consider your relationships right now what does that say about your relationship with Jesus Christ?

Perhaps some of what you are reading is leaving you discouraged. I hope that the fact that you have persevered to this point is an encouragement to you. Developing a deepening passion for Christ is not an instantaneous event. For most of us, certainly for me, it is a lifelong battle fraught with landmines of laziness, sneak attacks of sin, and sometimes agonizingly slow progress. What is most encouraging, however, is that God is fully committed to the growth of every one of His children. This is good news for me because it lets me know that my confidence is not ultimately in my strong grip on God, but in his strong grip on me. I hope you feel the same way.

As we read earlier in John 15, every one of God's children grows in reflecting the character of Christ in their lives in ever increasing degrees. Your transformation and growth in Christ is inextricably bound to the finished work of Christ! If you have given your life to Christ, you are not an orphan left to fend for yourself, but a child whose father is fully committed to your success. And your success, in knowing Him, in living for Him, and in glorifying Him with your life, is a manifestation of His glory that He will never give up on.

Maybe you are reading this and you are seriously questioning whether you have ever had a true change of heart, what the Bible calls being born again (John 3:3; 1 Pet. 1:3). If you think that is true, then right now could be the time for you to give your life wholly over to Jesus. To do this you need to do the following things (please also take a Bible and read each of the scriptures listed):

1. Acknowledge your sin and repent to God (see Rom. 3:23; 2 Cor. 7:10). This means that you are agreeing with God that you are a sinner. In addition you are repenting, which means that you are making a conscious decision to turn away from sin and towards God. In every area that you are aware of, you make it your intention to turn from those things that do not please God and live in a way that He will be glorified. Your acceptance by God is not based on doing this perfectly, but your desire to please Him in all things is a real indication that a true change has taken place in your life.

2. Put your faith in Jesus Christ alone for your salvation (see Rom. 6:23). This means that you now trust in nothing else to give you a right standing with God. You acknowledge that anything "good" that you have done is imperfect and worthless in terms of getting you right with God (see Isa. 64:6). You voluntarily give up your beliefs and practices that come from other religions, witchcraft, or occultic practices. Your hope for salvation is now based on Jesus' perfect sinless life, which He now credits to you, and His death on the cross that He suffered to pay for your sin (see 2 Cor. 5:21).

3. Confess with your mouth that Jesus Christ is Lord (see Rom. 10:9–10). Confessing Jesus' Lordship does not mean that by believing in Him you get a "get out of hell free card." It means that you acknowledge that He has a right over every area of your life and that He is indeed Lord over everything (see Col. 1:15–20). Your outward confession of this is an expression of your faith that acknowledges Jesus as Lord and Savior.

If you have just trusted in Jesus Christ for the first time, take time to pray and thank Him for salvation. Also make sure you begin reading your Bible regularly. I suggest starting with the gospel of Mark. In addition you need to get into a church that teaches the Bible and begin to build relationships with other believers. May the Lord bless you and be with you as begin to live your new life for Him.

Lord, I confess that I have allowed other things to take my time away from You. Help me, Lord, to make new decisions and to stop to be with You consistently through out my day, my week and my year. May time spent with You become the most important time in my day.

Grow me up in You so that my life will be used for Your glory and will be a blessing to those around me. I thank You, Lord, for strengthening me for this and I ask these things through Jesus Christ, to whom all glory, honor and praise is due. Amen.

4

MOVING FORWARD IN JESUS

A dead thing can go with the stream, but only a living thing can go against it.

—G.K. Chesterton

The movie *Napoleon Dynamite* tells the story of a strange family from Idaho with many bizarre eccentricities. One character from the movie, Uncle Rico, is a single, middle-aged man who is lost in the almost glory of his past. He dreams about his past as a high school quarterback who almost made it to the state finals, and who believes he could have been an NFL quarterback. Uncle Rico likes to consider time travel because he believes if he could just go back in time and change what happened in his last high school football game his whole life would be different and all his dreams would come true. Uncle Rico is totally lost in an unrealistic view of his past that does not allow him to live in the reality of his present. Because of this he has no real plan for the future, but only fantasies based on a distorted view of his past.[1]

There is probably an inner Uncle Rico in most of us. It is exceedingly easy to get lost in the past and to allow our regrets to move us to dream and fantasize and therefore not make any real progress in moving forward in life. When we live in gratitude and thanksgiving to God who allows us to work through the disappointments of our past, we are ready to live in the present with God and center our lives around a living relationship with Jesus Christ. A life centered in Jesus not only looks back to what He has done and stops now to be with Him, but also focuses on forward movement with Him as the center. The words of David in Psalm 37:3–4 are very instructive:

> Trust in the LORD, and do good;
> dwell in the land and befriend faithfulness.
> Delight yourself in the LORD,
> and he will give you the desires of your heart.

The first part of verse 3 is a wonderful summary of what life centered in Jesus looks like, "Trust in the Lord, and do good." To put this in the simplest terms possible we could say, "Trust and obey!" This is both simple and profound. Because we still deal with our sin nature every day our tendency is to make this very complicated. We easily confuse those areas where God calls us to trust Him and those areas where we are called to obey Him.

Like Adam and Eve after they fell into sin, we immediately cover up our nakedness in areas of our failure and then, like Adam, blame God and others for our own sin (see Gen. 3:12). We fail to obey God because we have given in to the implanted idea of the Enemy that God somehow is holding back from us and does not desire our good (see Gen. 3:1–7). When the serpent tells Eve in verse 5 that "God knows that when you eat of [the tree] your eyes will be opened and you will be like God, knowing good and evil," he is subtly telling her that God does not want what is best for her. This is the lie that continues to ensnare all of mankind. There is something out there apart from God that will give you what you really want—life!

TRUSTING IN GOD'S GOODNESS

The root of sin is the desire to find life apart from God. That is what led our first parents to turn away from trusting God. Where God is not trusted He will not be obeyed. It is impossible to walk in heart-level obedience to one you believe desires to harm you. Any outward obedience, perhaps gained by fear, is only a mask for an inward rebellion that ultimately desires to overthrow and bring down that ruthless authority. Sadly, much of what passes as obedience in many Christian circles is the result of this kind of fear that understands God not as a loving father but as powerful and unrestrained tyrant.

These verses in Psalm 37 are filled with commands of the Lord to His people. The very first command here is to trust (Hebrew: *batach*) in the Lord. This word connotes a confident hope and expectation.[2] Here believers are instructed to put all of their hope in Yahweh. Unlike the gods of the surrounding nations who were capricious and fickle, the God of Israel is steadfast and faithful. Therefore, as the people of Yahweh, it is reasonable in every way to trust in Him. Interestingly, when this word is translated into Greek in the Septuagint (a translation of the Hebrew Bible from the second century BC) it is never translated with the word for faith (*pistis*) but always with the word for hope (*elpis*). The nuance here is that trusting God means looking forward to what He will do and resting in the assurance of His proven character.

Coupled with the command to trust in Yahweh is the command to "do good." The ability to do good is intimately connected with knowing that Yahweh is in control and the belief that He is acting for our good. This is the reversal of Genesis 3. The sin of Genesis 3 was a rebellious unwillingness to trust in Yahweh that led to the fall. The redeemed community is called to live out of the knowledge of the Lord's faithfulness and therefore to follow His commandments.

FEEDING ON FAITHFULNESS

As is normal in Hebrew poetry, the second part of the verse reinforces and deepens the first part: "Dwell in the land and befriend faithfulness." Although the verbs used are still commands, the idea is also clothed in one of deepest promises of the Old Testament. From Abram's initial call in Genesis 12 to Moses' call in Exodus 3, God's people were promised a land that would be theirs. Dwelling in the land is the quintessential manifestation the Lord's faithfulness to them. They are not, however, merely called to be those who inhabit the land, but those who will live consciously under the care of their faithful provider. The language used here is very compelling. The word translated "befriend" in the ESV (Hebrew: *ra'ah*) is primarily used for the work of a shepherd who tends to his flock.[3] The idea is that the flock is enabled to eat or graze and thus enjoy the benefits of fertile land.

Of course the object of shepherding here is not a flock of sheep. The instruction is to graze on faithfulness. Whose faithfulness is this speaking of? Most likely it is the faithfulness of the Lord who has given them the land in the first place. The idea is that God's people move forward by trusting in Him and living in all the benefits of his promises. They are able to live in the land he has provided and feed off of His faithfulness as their sustenance.

This is the essence of what it means to move forward in Christ. The hymn writer said it well, "Christ is my meat; He is my drink, my medicine and my health, my portion, my inheritance, yea all my boundless wealth!"[4] To move forward in Jesus is to feed on Him daily. We feed on His faithfulness. We pasture in the place of His abundance. In a fallen world, and living in flawed and sin-filled bodies, we must graze on our all-sufficient savior. To feed on Him is to have every necessary life-sustaining nutrient.

DELIGHTING IN THE LORD

Verse 4 continues the pattern of command and promise: "Delight yourself in the Lord and he will give you the desires of your heart." The Hebrew word translated "delight" (*anog*) means to take exquisite delight in something.[5] We are being commanded here to enjoy God! In one sense it would seem that there is no easier command in all the Scripture. Since we were made to enjoy Him this is the most natural of all things to do, or so it would seem. But our experience and the plain record of Scripture tells us a different story. From the time of the fall of our first parents into sin, we have all looked everywhere else but to the Lord to find satisfaction and enjoyment.

The truth is that we cannot and we will not turn from satisfying ourselves with sin unless we make Jesus the object or our exquisite delight. Our lesser affections, ruled by the unrelenting impurity of our flesh, do not give way unless forcibly removed by a greater affection. For this reason we are commanded to delight in the Lord! To do this is a fight that requires us to be tenacious about finding our satisfaction in the Lord, and this is ground zero in the battle for our hearts and therefore our lives.

Because of the corruption of our flesh, we live as if we have been dipped in a vat of glue that attracts to itself all things impure and ungodly. It takes no effort on our part; we merely need to breathe and live to find corruption clinging tightly to us. Furthermore this outward sticky coat that attracts and welcomes sin, our flesh, is not going away anytime soon. What hope then are we left with to make any progress in godliness in this life?

We are left with the hope of the living Christ! The work of Christ in the believer's life is one that works from the inside out. As we feast on Him and delight in Him, it is as if our outward shell, which was once magnetized to attract every ungodly thing, now repulses those exact same things. As we delight ourselves in the Lord, our thinking and our passions become realigned with His. This is why He is able to promise in the second part of the verse that, "He will give you the desires of your heart." It is not that we have somehow manipulated God by an outward act of piety in such a way that He is now obligated to cave into our demands. On the contrary, it is we who have "caved in"! We have been changed and renewed to now desire the very things that are closest to the heart of God.

RADICAL REALIGNMENT

This type of radical realignment of desires and passions is demonstrated powerfully in the life of the apostle Paul. In Second Corinthians 5:14 he says of himself and his partners, "For the love of Christ controls us, because we have concluded this: that one has died for all, therefore all have died." Paul is declaring here that the direction of his life and the daily decisions he makes are guided by one overarching reality—the love of Christ. This phrase, the love of Christ, can mean either the love that Christ has for us or the love that we have for Christ. In all reality the phrase means both of these things.

Paul is stating here that he is overwhelmed as he considers how God has loved him. He understands that Jesus, the second person of the eternal Godhead, decided to take on a new nature and become a man. He decided to live a perfect life and to die in our place for our sins. Paul understands that Jesus Christ took upon Himself the punishment for our sin, which is nothing less than the holy wrath of God, in order that we might be spared. He understands furthermore that Jesus has given those who believe in Him credit for all His perfect righteousness in spite of their ongoing record of sin and unrighteousness.

With all of these facts in Paul is floored. He is taken aback by the wonder of God's grace which is perfectly revealed in Jesus. And he is controlled or compelled by this in every area of his life. The Greek word used here for control is *sunecho*. This word can refer to something being literally held together.[6] Negatively this word is sometimes used to indicate someone being enclosed or locked up as a prisoner. It means that the subject is powerfully constrained in what they are able to do by someone or something else.

This is exactly how Paul sees Christ's love. Because he is grasping this love, and therefore delighting in Christ, his movements and decisions are highly constrained. He does not experience this as imprisonment, however, but as liberation. His life is controlled by Christ's love in such a way that all of his efforts are put forth to demonstrate Christ's love to others and to compel them to be reconciled to God (see 2 Cor. 5:18–20). He has been set free, as it were, from the fleshly passions that once had control of him, in order that he might now be and instrument of God's grace in the lives of others.

Thomas Chalmers, the nineteenth-century Scottish preacher and church leader, famously preached a sermon entitled *The Expulsive Power of a New Affection*.[7] The idea of this sermon is that we do not defeat or overcome our habits, addictions and worldly passions by self-will or determination, but by having developed a yet greater affection that is able to expel that which is weaker. This is the challenge and the aim of making Christ central. When we value him rightly for who He is, our lesser affections are able to be forcibly overcome by our increased affection for Christ. This is what Paul is speaking about experiencing in his own life in Second Corinthians 5.

JESUS ON CENTER STAGE

This is what it means to move forward in Christ. As believers we feed off of His grace, His righteousness, His love and all of His perfections in such a way that we are empowered to live for Him. We are all in need of constant self-evaluation in this regard. Can you honestly conclude that love for Christ is the dominating reality of your life? Stop here and consider this more deeply. I would encourage you to take some time at this point to prayerfully journal on two thoughts:

1. Does the way that I think and live center around the person of Jesus Christ?
2. In what ways is God calling me at this time to live differently so that Jesus will become more central in every facet of my thoughts and actions?

I encourage you to take fifteen to twenty minutes to think through these questions and write down your thoughts. Write out both positive and negative things from question one. Think creatively in question two about small ways in which you can make Jesus more central to your everyday life.

Let's think back to Uncle Rico. He was lost in a view of glory where he was established as the centerpiece. His ultimate desire to go back and change history was tied to his wish to bring greater glory and comfort to himself and therefore be celebrated by others.[8] I struggle daily with my inner Uncle Rico that desires to have myself celebrated and glorified more than Jesus. Only by grasping the truth of the gospel does my self-absorbed passion begin to give way. As the gospel of Jesus begins to fill in the cracks and crevices of my heart, I see a greater passion for His glory becoming a more the consuming reality in my life. With this my soul begins to sing out, with the apostle and all the saints, "Oh the depth of the riches and wisdom and knowledge of God! How unsearchable are his judgments and how inscrutable are his ways!" (Rom. 11:33). Jesus takes His rightful place, replacing me as the center of my affections. Therefore my life becomes what it was meant to be from the beginning— a conduit to show of the glory of God!

We have now taken four chapters to establish that we must make knowing Jesus Christ the first priority in our upward movement to establish him as the center of our lives. God's love for us is most powerfully demonstrated through the incarnation, life, death and resurrection of his unique son, Jesus Christ. To move towards God we move towards Jesus Christ. In reality the incarnation of Christ tells us beyond all doubt that God is moving towards us. Immanuel is here.

O Lord God, creator, redeemer and lover of our souls, We declare that You alone are the source of all life. Forgive us for looking for life, purpose and joy apart from You.

Help us to know that apart from You there is no hope, no power, no direction and no good thing.

Increase our desire to delight in You and You alone to find what we desperately need.

We ask this through our Lord Jesus Christ, Your Son, Who lives and reigns with You and the Holy Spirit, One God, forever and ever. Amen.

5

LIFE EMPOWERED BY THE HOLY SPIRIT

My trust in God flows out of the experience of his loving me, day in and day out, whether the day is stormy or fair, whether I'm sick or in good health, whether I'm in a state of grace or disgrace. He comes to me where I live and loves me as I am.

—Brennan Manning

Several years ago my wife had open-heart surgery. She never had a heart attack, but began to have some significant symptoms. One Saturday morning as we finished eating breakfast at a local diner she could barely walk and was finding it hard to breathe. We went immediately to the hospital emergency room and they hooked her up to machines and quickly had doctors working with her. We were scared, anxious and very confused as we saw the rush of doctors as Harriette struggled hard to get her breath.

As her symptoms subsided we were grateful to hear that she had not had a heart attack. They kept her overnight to do more tests and before discharge we met with the cardiologist. They had run several EKGs during her stay and, based on that, he was happy to tell us that although he could not say exactly what it was, he could confidently say that it was not her heart. We were enormously relieved. He did indicate that there was one other test that she should have done but she could do that later. We went home, got on a bunch of medical websites, diagnosed what we thought the problem was and went on with life. We made an appointment for the other test, a stress test, and went about life.

The next week we went to the doctor's office to do the stress test. Within thirty seconds the doctor noticed there was something significantly wrong. This time we were shaken to the core. He brought both of us into his office and told us that she would very likely need open heart surgery. Minutes earlier we were planning out our weekend without a care in the world and now we were told she needed open heart surgery immediately or she could very well die. Within minutes our whole world had turned upside down and we did our best to gather ourselves emotionally and remember that Jesus was still in control.

In a final diagnostic test before the surgery we learned that her condition was rare but often fatal. She had blocked arteries but none of the blockages in and of themselves was very significant. Because of this they were missed on most of the tests. The issue was not the degree of any of the blockages but the pattern of the blockages on her artery. The doctor told us that the pattern is referred to as the "widow maker" because it often results in a person having minimal symptoms until they have a lethal heart attack. The cumulative effect of the blockages only showed up when the heart was under stress from physical or emotional exertion. Under those conditions blood was effectively cut off from the heart and then the fatal attack could take place.

My wife's mother had died from a massive heart attack at the age of forty-two and Harriette had inherited this condition. Words can never express how thankful we are that Harriette did have symptoms that showed up and likely kept her from having a massive heart attack. The combination of multiple "minor" blockages and physical and/or emotional stress was a time bomb that could have exploded at any time. The Lord has surely been gracious to us.

SPIRITUAL BLOCKAGES

Without proper blood flow to the heart physical life is impossible. This experience powerfully taught Harriette and me that there are many ways, even subtle ways, to cut off the flow of blood that is necessary for life. As a believer in Jesus Christ, the Holy Spirit is the one who enables us to be connected to the person of Jesus Christ. Sometimes it is only the stress tests of life that reveal whether we have a vital and authentic relationship with Jesus. What we may think of as a healthy connection may be revealed as defective when we are broadsided by trials and difficulties. As you consider recent trials that you have faced, what have they revealed to you about the strength of your connection to Jesus? Are there blockages that need to be addressed?

Real life—vital connection with Jesus Christ—only comes by the power and person of the Holy Spirit. Many people who call themselves Christians have a woefully deficient understanding of the work of the Holy Spirit. This results, for the most part, from an unbiblical understanding of what salvation is in the first place. Very often this is a view of salvation that highlights the activity and emotions of human beings but does not look at salvation from the Divine perspective. When we do not begin to understand the work of the Holy Spirit in salvation, we are left in a precarious position. If salvation is simply a result of a man-made decision then there would appear to be no real place of security in our salvation.

Evangelical Christianity has popularized the idea of making "a personal decision for Christ." Of course the Bible does teach that each individual is accountable to God and must willingly submit their life to God. We are called to make a personal decision to accept Jesus Christ. We need to be careful, however, when we use the language of a "personal decision." Too often this language carries with it the idea that salvation is granted solely on the basis of what we do as if God has nothing to do with it. The work of God in the human heart has effectively been taken out of the equation. Understood this way, the "personal decision" can be thought of much like the famous line from the poem *Invictus* by William Earnest Henley[1]: "I am the master of my fate, I am the captain of my soul."

The problem is that the Bible knows nothing of this type of grandiose thought. The first stanza of the poem reads as follows:

> Out of the night that covers me,
> Black as the pit from pole to pole,
> I thank whatever gods may be,
> For my unconquerable soul.[2]

No doubt that many people have been inspired by this poem over the years and many have even tried to read into its meaning a Christian worldview. However, the ability to do this only reveals how unbiblical our worldview actually is! The believer does not suppose that he has any such thing as an "unconquerable soul," or that he should in any way be the master of his fate or the captain of his soul. In fact, the Christian worldview obliterates this type of thinking.

The hymn writer put it this way:

> My hope is built on nothing less than Jesus' blood and righteousness;

> I dare not trust the sweetest frame, but wholly lean on Jesus' name.
> On Christ, the solid Rock, I stand; all other ground is sinking sand.[3]

Forsaking faith in self we learn to lean wholly on the grace of God! The Lord's promise to His children is exactly this: "I am with you always" (Matt. 28:20)! In this verse Jesus is assuring His people that they do not need to depend on anything or anyone else—indeed they are forbidden to do so. Specifically, believers are to not put their confidence in self. This idea is summed up well in the first commandment, "I am the Lord your God who brought you out of the land of Egypt, out of the house of slavery. You shall have no other gods before me" (Exod. 20:2–3).

Now if this were all that the Bible had to say about this we might find ourselves in some serious trouble. It is one thing to be told not to rely on anything or anyone else, but quite another to live that way when life becomes difficult (and it always becomes difficult). Thankfully the full weight of Scripture describes the unfolding of God's covenantal care for His children. As our good shepherd (Ps. 23:1; John 10:11), our rock and fortress (Ps. 31:3), our wonderful counselor (Isa. 9:7), our strength and shield (Ps. 28:7) and our only hope (39:7; 62:5), the Lord demonstrates both in precept and deed that He alone is sufficient to meet our deepest needs.

THE BATTLE FOR CONTROL

As fallen creatures, however, we constantly battle to find our identity and direction from sources other than the Living God. The essence of the first act of sin by Adam and Eve in the garden was this: to declare their independence from God. It was not just a random tree that they were forbidden to eat from, but "the tree of the knowledge of good and evil" (Gen. 2:17). Not eating from this tree was an ongoing demonstration of their reliance upon God to instruct them day-by-day. They understood that they needed to hear from God every day and receive His wisdom in order to carry out their daily tasks in ruling over the created order to glorify Him (see 1:28).

The Bible gives us a beautiful picture of God meeting with Adam and Eve by walking in the garden in the cool of the day (3:8). This seems to have been the normal occurrence before their fall into sin. God walks with them, instructs them and loves them through His presence with them. They are abiding under the shadow of His wings with no inward compulsion toward sin. And yet in spite of having every benefit that we can imagine, they choose to rebel against the Lord in order to decide for themselves what is good and what is evil. They rebel against the one and only commandment God gave them and thus propel not only themselves but all mankind into the life and death struggle with sin.

This is the unrelenting and potentially life-dominating enemy that seeks to eradicate the true knowledge of God and ultimately destroy every vestige of hope from the human heart. Sin makes the easy promise of life and autonomy from God's rule, but produces death and slavery to every ungodly vice that so easily captivates our fallen hearts. Sin always brings forth death (James 1:15).

Against the backdrop of this reality Jesus comes into the world and demonstrates the power of God to obliterate the dominance of sin. His disciples watch in wonder as He raises the dead, gives sight to the blind, calms the wind and waves and multiplies food for thousands. He teaches with authority that no one had ever seen before and demons tremble and flee in his presence. Surely they believe that it is just a matter of time until Jesus brings down every ungodly and oppressive structure and sets up His permanent kingdom on the earth.

In the middle of this whirlwind of ministry and unprecedented power Jesus seemingly demolishes His disciples hopes with these words, "It is best for you that I go away" (John 16:7, NLT). *WHAT! How can this be?* The grieving disciples can grasp neither the power nor the necessity of these words. Jesus continues by saying, " . . . because if I don't [go away] the Advocate will not come. If I do go away then I will send him to you" (16:7, NLT).

Earlier in this same discourse with the disciples, Jesus had spoken these words regarding the Holy Spirit: "The world cannot receive him, because it isn't looking for him and doesn't recognize him. But you know him, because he lives with you now and later will be in you" (14:17, NLT). The end of this verse is critical—"he lives with you now and later will be in you." This is the key to understanding how it could possibly be better for the disciples for Jesus to go away. Jesus is saying that the person of the Holy Spirit is *with* them now because of His (Jesus') presence *with* them, but when Jesus goes away the same Holy Spirit will live *in* them! This is the promised outpouring of the Holy Spirit on the church that occurred on the day of Pentecost. This is the same Holy Spirit who dwells in the heart of every true believer.

OUR NEED FOR THE HOLY SPIRIT

The reality of a Christ-centered life presupposes the presence of the Holy Spirit in the believer. If there is no Holy Spirit there is no hope, no conversion, no new life, and no power to overcome sin. Paul puts it this way in Romans 8:9: "Anyone who does not have the Spirit of Christ does not belong to him." It is clear within the context of Romans that "the Spirit of Christ" is equated with the Holy Spirit. Paul is therefore saying here that anyone who professes to be a Christian, but does not have the Holy Spirit, is actually not a believer at all.

This makes perfect sense to anyone who has grappled with depth of their own sinfulness. It is absurd to think that I can make any progress in holiness in this world without the power of another at work in me. And that other must be one who is Himself both holy and powerful. There is only one who meets that criteria. It is not "my higher power" but the Holy Spirit of God—the third person of the Trinity. The great news for believers is that He is the promised possession of everyone who calls on the name of Jesus in humble repentance.

Paul uses these words to describe the gift of the Holy Spirit to believers: "It is God who enables us, along with you, to stand firm for Christ. He has commissioned us, and he has identified us as His own by placing the Holy Spirit in our hearts as the *first installment that guarantees everything he has promised us*" (2 Cor. 1:21–22, NLT). The Holy Spirit stands as the first installment or down payment that God Himself makes to guarantee that all His promises will be fully manifested in the lives of his children.

A down payment is a common term in real estate transactions. The down payment is a promise that allows the one who pays it to be said to "own" the property even though they need to continue to pay for it—sometimes for thirty more years! When the down payment is accepted by the bank, it gives over the rights as property owners to the one who has paid them to the degree that they are now fully responsible for the property.

I live in Philadelphia. One of the important implications of home ownership is that I need to maintain the property in such a way that it does not pose a hazard to anyone who happens to be on the property. In my city some people (and some lawyers) make a living through fraudulent injury claims for slipping and falling on sidewalks and steps and then suing property owners for their negligence. Even though I may owe 90 percent of the value of the property to the bank and they can take the property from me if I miss a few payments, I am the one responsible for the property. When someone falls they sue me and not the bank. It is an interesting position to be put in. I am fully responsible as an owner and yet the bank can easily and legally take over the ownership if I fail in my promise to pay the rest. In reality, as long as I owe the bank I am a co-owner at best, but held responsible by others as if I were the sole owner.

Thanks be to God that He has never defaulted on a loan! His down payment of the Holy Spirit is not a partial payment in the way that my down payment is. As a matter of fact, it is not really a payment at all. The full payment for my sin has already been accomplished by the work of Christ. He shouts in triumph from the cross, "It is finished!" (John 19:30). There is nothing more to be paid because Jesus paid it all.

What then do we mean by saying that the Holy Spirit is a down payment that guarantees that God will fully complete His work in the life of a believer? Simply this: that the presence of the Holy Spirit in a person's life is the manifest evidence that the person is a child of God. By pouring out the Holy Spirit on the believer, God has given the tangible, inescapable proof of His full ownership of the life of the believer.

EVIDENCE OF THE HOLY SPIRIT

To say that this evidence is "tangible and inescapable" implies that it can be seen. On one hand this statement could be easily refuted. I have never "seen" the Holy Spirit. He is not an appendage to the person in the way that an arm or leg is. I get no clue to His presence by hair color, body type, ethnic identity or any other outward physical characteristic.

On the other hand the Scriptures give us abundant tangible evidence of the presence of the Holy Spirit. Specifically we see the Holy Spirit manifested through the fruit of the Spirit which is outlined in Galatians 5:22–23. The growing presence of explicitly Christ-inspired love, joy, peace, patience, kindness, goodness, faithfulness, gentleness and self-control is tangible evidence of the presence of the Holy Spirit in a person's life. Jesus said that you shall know a tree by its fruit (see Matt. 7:15–23). It is not giftedness or extraordinary acts of ministry—"Did we not cast out demons in your name?"; but the undeniable reality of a life that is conformed more and more to the life of Jesus. This fruit—as tangible as the apple on an apple tree—shows off the reality of the Holy Spirit at work in the life of every true believer. Because of the indwelling presence of the Holy Spirit, it is impossible to truly believe in Jesus Christ and not be progressively transformed more and more into His image.

In Ephesians, Paul compares the influence of the Holy Spirit on the life of a believer to the effect of being intoxicated with wine: "And do not get drunk with wine, for that is debauchery, but be filled with the Spirit" (Eph. 5:18). There are some obvious parallels here. Being inebriated with alcohol has several unmistakable effects. First of all, your speech is slurred and you can no longer speak the same way as when you were sober. The believer, filled with Holy Spirit, also has a distinctly changed pattern of communication. The following verses outline how Spirit-filled believers communicate in psalms, hymns and spiritual songs and continually give thanks to God for everything in the name of the Lord Jesus Christ.

Of course this does not mean that believers go around singing "How Great Thou Art" all day. It does mean that under the influence of the Holy Spirit my speech honors and reverences God, builds up my brothers and sisters and constantly gives thanks for all He has done. It is also significant that verse 20 indicates that all of this is done in the name of the Lord Jesus Christ. Spirit-filled believers cannot keep the name of the Lord who has saved them off of their lips. Because the Holy Spirit works in a way perfectly united to Jesus, believers are not just generally grateful to an unnamed deity, but specifically giving glory, honor and praise to the Lord Jesus Christ.

Secondly, being drunk has the effect of significantly impairing one's ability to walk. When someone is heavily under the influence of alcohol it is impossible to walk as if one was sober. Without question the work of the Holy Spirit forever changes the walk of the believer. Even as Jacob was never able to walk the same way after he wrestled with the preincarnate Christ in Genesis 32, so also the Spirit-filled believer can no longer walk in the same way. Does this mean that Christians no longer sin? Of course not! However, it does mean that it is now impossible to continue in sin without undergoing both the conviction that the Holy Spirit gives (see John 16:8) and the discipline that the Father gives (see Heb. 12:5–11). Positively, it also means that over time the believer will make progress in their walk with God in a way that gives great glory to God.

One word of warning is important. Progress over time may not look like we think it should at any given point in time. That is to say that there will be set backs, lapses of faith, long-term struggles with specific sins and times where it is hard to tell the believer from the unbeliever. However, these things do not define the believer! It is the reality of the power of the indwelling Spirit of God that gradually shapes every part of the life and walk of God's children. Because of the indwelling Holy Spirit, God's children are stamped with His likeness and will progressively show forth their family resemblance. More and more they will look like their daddy! More and more they will look like their older brother!

DIVINE PERSPECTIVE

This is so often misunderstood because salvation has been understood from an exclusively human perspective. It is true that salvation is manifested in time as a person believes in Jesus Christ and makes a profession of faith in Him. However, the Bible talks about this process as being "born again" (John 3:3; 1 Pet. 1:23). What is outwardly manifested in belief and profession is first birthed inside as the Holy Spirit invades the inner world of the person and changes them from the inside out. Jesus description of this in John 3 using the analogy of normal human birth is very instructive. No woman, however fertile, can conceive without the sperm being implanted into her body from the outside. There is nothing inside of her that can produce life without a life-giving invasion.

Understood this way, it becomes clear that spiritual life is only made possible by the invasive work of the Holy Spirit. He is, as the Nicene Creed[4] states, "The Lord, the giver of life." The agent of life-transforming power is not the will of man manipulated by persuasive words but the power of the living God now occupying every crack and crevice of the human heart. With this understanding it becomes clear that real spiritual life is totally dependent upon the presence of the Holy Spirit. If He is not present, there is no life. This is why the apostle says later that, "Anyone who does not have the Spirit of Christ does not belong to him" (Rom. 8:9).

All of this begs the question, "How then do I get the Holy Spirit in my life?" The answer may seem circular but it is simple: You are never commanded to *get the Holy Spirit* in your life. You are commanded to *believe in Jesus Christ* and submit to Him as your Lord. When you do this and grow in your love and appreciation for Him as your life is progressively transformed, you can know for certain that the Holy Spirit is at work in your life. You know the tree came from an apple seed because it produces the right fruit—apples. In the same way, you know that a person has the Holy Spirit because their life consistently manifests fruit congruent with that reality.

This truth is summed up well in First Corinthians 12:13 where we read, "For in one Spirit we were all baptized into one body—Jews or Greeks, slave or free—and all were made to drink of one Spirit." Being baptized by the Holy Spirit is not the exclusive right of a certain sect of Christians but the birthright of every believer.

YEILDING TO THE HOLY SPIRIT

One last issue must be addressed as we speak about our need to rely on the power of the Holy Spirit in our lives. The verse in Ephesians 5:18 that we looked at earlier urges believers not to get drunk on wine but "to be filled with the Holy Spirit." This is given to believers as a command, that is, something that they are responsible to do. On the face of it this may seem to directly contradict what we have just spoken of above. This, however, is not the case at all.

As we have said, believers are not urged to "get the Holy Spirit," as if they do not have Him in their lives. As we have seen, no one can believe in Jesus as the Christ and give their lives to Him without the work of the Holy Spirit within them. On the other hand, believers are responsible to daily yield themselves to the work of the Holy Spirit who has been given to them.

Being filled with the Spirit does not imply getting something or someone that I do not have, but rather, daily yielding my life to the power of the Holy Spirit who lives within me. The command in Romans 6:13 to "present yourselves to God as those who have been brought from death to life, and your members to God as instruments for righteousness," is the command to yield to the work of the Holy Spirit who lives in you. No one has the power to do this of themselves. The means of obeying the command given in Romans 6 is more fully explained by the role of the Holy Spirit outlined in Romans 8.

This is also why the passage in Romans 7:7–25 which speaks of the futility of escaping a life of sin never once mentions the work of the Holy Spirit! This passage does not describe the normal Christian life at all as many have taught. It describes life under the yoke of the law and without the life-giving, yoke-destroying power of God's Spirit at work in a person's life. Life in the Spirit, described in Romans 8, is the life that demolishes the work of the Enemy and conforms us to the image of Jesus Christ.

What does this have to say about how I practically live out my life as a believer? It means that the Christian life is one of learning to yield on a more consistent basis to the power of the Holy Spirit. I remember as a young believer desperately seeking for the key thing that I could discover that would change me forever. By this type of change I really meant having freedom from the ongoing and sometimes life debilitating temptations that plagued me and caused me to fall into sin once again. What I was really asking for was that my flesh would be changed. Over the course of time I came to realize this shocking truth—this is nowhere on God's agenda for this age! Flesh will always be flesh and will always be in opposition to God wanting to gratify itself. It will not improve, develop, progress or be made better in any way.

This is why believers stand in desperate need of relying on the power of the Holy Spirit in order to live a Christ-centered life. The weakness, frailty and ongoing mess that is my flesh serves as the God-ordained background for the glorious work of the Holy Spirit. Christ's glory is manifested in high definition to all of creation as the Holy Spirit conforms me to His image in spite of this weak, sinful, and self-absorbed thing that is my flesh.

REDEEMING SIN

Remarkably, the selfish me-worship of my flesh is an integral part of the "all things" in Romans 8:28 that work to the good and maximizes the glory of Jesus Christ in His creation. God reveals Himself as the Redeemer—the great Redeemer! Against all odds, all logic, all powers of darkness and every evil thing that is allied in an all-out war to destroy, marginalize and devastate any vestige of God's glory in my life—God Redeems. His redemption is not just seen in the forgiveness of my sin but in the transforming work of the Holy Spirit that molds me progressively more into the image of the Jesus Christ.

The essence of the Christ-centered life is this: the Holy Spirit filling every part of the life of God's children so that that the aroma of Christ is unmistakably and consistently present. Our flesh consistently stands as the "widow maker" attempting to bring sudden death by cutting us off from vital connection to Christ. Against this, however, the Holy Spirit comes to bring us life by keeping us closely tethered to Jesus.

Practical directives for living a life that increasingly yields itself to the power of the Holy Spirit include:

1. Declaring your total inability to please God or live for Him based on your own ability and strength.
2. Thanking God for the gift of the person of the Holy Spirit at work in your life. (Please remember that the Holy Spirit is not a force or power that emanates from God but is Himself a person.)
3. Asking God to help you to focus your mind on Jesus today and consciously yield your mind and body to the Holy Spirit consistently.
4. Taking time to stop, focus on Jesus and ask the Holy Spirit to give you strength when you are in a particularly challenging or tempting situation.

In this we see one of the great mysteries of the gospel at work—we are only strong when we know just how weak we really are (see 2 Cor. 12:9). The wonder of it all is this: the strength we are given is not through some steroid that helps to grow our muscles bigger but the very power of God Himself at work in us by the Holy Spirit! It is this reality that even the angels of heaven long to understand (see 1 Pet. 1:12).

O Lord, I am undressed before You.
You see my naked sin and my ugly obsession with self.
Even my desire to honor You meets with no power from self, and no help from this world.

But I praise You, O Lord, that You have not left me to myself, nor to the devices of this world.
I thank You, Lord God, that You have deposited Your Spirit within me,
and given me life and strength by
Your Holy Spirit.

Help me, O Lord, to yield all that I am and all that I desire this day to the blessed Holy Spirit.
This I ask through Jesus, the Christ,
to whom alone belongs all glory, honor and praise,
both now and forevermore. Amen.

6

LIFE SUBMITTED TO THE WORD OF GOD

"Like a tree planted by streams of water" (Ps. 1:3), the soul is irrigated by the Bible and acquires vigor, produces tasty fruit, namely, true faith, and is beautified with a thousand green leaves, namely, actions that please God. The Bible, in fact, leads us towards pure holiness and holy actions. In it we find encouragement to all the virtues and the warning to flee from evil.

—John of Damascus

"Food is meant for the stomach and the stomach for food" (1 Cor. 6:13). This was apparently a proverb that was spoken in Corinth that instructed people that if they have a physical urge they should always do what it takes to satisfy that urge. Although this is not how God instructs us to make decisions regarding our desires and passions, most of us can relate to the power of this proverb. I have never been really good at fasting. I do it from time to time, but honestly, it takes a great deal of effort and it is hard for me. It is a necessary and important spiritual discipline but one that takes a great deal of focus and effort for me to accomplish.

From time to time I run into professional fasters. Perhaps you've run into them as well. Someone offhandedly talks about "coming off a forty-day fast" in the way that I would talk about driving home from work. My first reaction is shame and then anger as I think about how hard it was for me to skip two meals last Wednesday. Something inside of me—I'm certain it's not the Holy Spirit—wants to slap them, but I get myself together enough to calmly reply, "Oh that's wonderful! How do you sense the Lord directing you through this?"

Fasting is an important and difficult spiritual discipline because by it we deny ourselves one of the most basic needs and wants that we have. Most of us quickly feel the effects of fasting because our bodies are craving needed nutrition and calories so that we can have energy to perform our daily functions. This is why fasting was never meant to be the normal everyday lifestyle of a believer. It is an interruption to the normal so that our attention can be focused acutely on God.

Over time none of us will do very well without something in our stomach. The reality is that we will not live very long if we don't eat. Life is contingent upon putting the right food into our bodies on a consistent basis in order to sustain our vital systems and organs. Occasional fasting is helpful, but without an ongoing diet of healthy food our bodies will quickly waste away.

THE BELIEVERS' DIET

What is true in the natural is also true in the spiritual. The Christ-centered life cannot be maintained without the proper diet. For believers who have access to the Bible in a language that they understand, this must include consistently reading the Word of God. To neglect reading the Scriptures when they are easily available to you is the spiritual equivalent of going on a suicidal hunger strike. The Word of God, the Bible, is real food that is designed by God to bring spiritual nutrition to every crack and crevice of the believing soul.

The singular importance of the discipline cannot be overstated. Reading the Bible cannot and must not be relegated to one item on a spiritual disciplines menu. One person connects with God through nature—that is great. Another person connects with God in deep relationships with people—that is great. However, whatever your personal wiring is, no one who has the ability to read and the access to a Bible can say, "I'm not much of a reader so I'll connect with God in other ways." Reading the Bible consistently with an open heart that is seeking for God is the greatest spiritual multivitamin that God has blessed His people to possess.

One morning I woke up to my wife moving about and getting ready to go to work. I wondered how well she had slept so I said to her, "How are you doing this morning?" She gave me the answer that every man dreads. "You know," she said, and then she added the clincher, "exegete me!" My immediate emotional response was terror. "Oh gosh," I thought, "What is this woman talking about?" As those words came out of her mouth I had no idea. The previous night we had met with a couple that we were mentoring through our premarital class at church and I was speaking to him about the importance of "exegeting your wife." I spoke passionately about his need to study her closely so he can know what she is thinking and feeling in order to care for her well. Now the worm had turned!

By God's good grace I quickly remembered what was happening that day that had my wife's emotional attention. She had a doctor's appointment later that day and she was concerned about it. I think I recovered in a way that she did not perceive my terror, but for that split second my terror was very real. Had I not remembered what was going on with my wife that day it would not have been good for me! She had a reasonable expectation that I should know her enough to understand what was deeply troubling her. Thank You, Jesus, for helping me to remember just in time!

The idea of a husband needing to know his wife well is a foundational biblical idea when it comes to marriage. "Husbands, live with your wives in an understanding way" (1 Pet. 3:7) or "dwell with them according to knowledge" (KJV). The idea is that if a man is to love his wife well, he must spend the time, effort and attention to work at knowing her deeply. It is not enough to provide and produce—husbands are called to understand and empathize. In the absence of this, the Scripture says that if a man is not honoring his wife, then God will not hear his prayers (see 3:7).

GOD'S INVITATION

If God calls a husband to know his wife well—and He does—how much more is a believer to know his Lord well? If my wife has a valid expectation that I should know what is troubling her heart, how much more should God expect me to know what troubles His heart? From the beginning, God's intention in creating man was to develop an intimate relationship where men and women knew God deeply.

To know God, to really know Him, is the greatest pleasure of life. To understand His ways and His thoughts more accurately is the blessed privilege of believers. Of course our knowledge of God will never be comprehensive because He is inexhaustible in His infinite glory. However, the glorious, almighty, infinite, creator and redeemer of the universe woos His people into an ever-increasing knowledge of His eternal glory so that they might proclaim His glory to a watching world. What a privilege, blessing and honor to be called to spend our lives glorifying the King of Glory!

"The heavens declare the glory of God," David says, "and the sky above proclaims his handiwork" (Ps. 19:1). To see nature, both the vastness of the universe and the intricacies of the smallest cell, is to get a glimpse of just how great God is. And yet all of nature's glories are not enough to even begin to give us the depth of knowledge that God desires us to have.

David goes on to say in Psalm 19:7, "The law of the LORD is perfect, reviving the soul." Ah . . . now here is something infinitely greater than the witness of the heavens—God's word! David refers to God's law as the one thing that is able to give life to the soul. In another place the psalmist says, "Your word is a lamp to my feet and a light to my path" (119:105). Just two verses later he declares, "I am severely afflicted; give me life, O LORD, according to your word!" (119:107). Life, true life, is bound up in the Word of God. The upward movement of a believer seeking to connect directly to God demands that the believer pay close attention to His word. Apart from developing a growing knowledge of God *through the Bible itself*, the believer will not mature and his or her growth will be severely stunted. This is a tragedy of the highest magnitude because it means that a vessel specifically designed to shine light on the glorious God is not able to do so. Therefore, the upward movement that bids us to make Jesus the center of our lives and to rely on the empowering work of the Holy Spirit, must necessarily be informed by an accurate and growing knowledge of the Word of God—the Bible.

WHY THE BIBLE?

The Bible is unique. There is no other thing like it in the world. The Bible is the authoritative Word of God that has been preserved throughout the centuries by God so that his people will know him. Second Timothy 3:16–17 (NIV) says, "All Scripture is God-breathed and is useful for teaching, rebuking, correcting and training in righteousness, so that the servant of God may be thoroughly equipped for every good work." The Greek word rendered "God-breathed" in the NIV translation (and breathed out by God in the ESV) is the word '*theopnevstos*.' The Expositors Bible Commentary points out that this adjective is actually a compound of *theos*, "God" and the verb *pneo*, "breath."[1] Some of the older translations use words like "inspired by God," but "God-breathed" is actually a better translation.

We can use the word "inspired" in any number of ways to indicate that something had some mysterious and wonderful creative power behind it. A song, a poem or even an idea for marketing a product can be said to be "inspired." Being "God-breathed", however, is something altogether different. By using this particular word, the Holy Spirit is conveying to God's people that the words of Scripture are the very words of God Himself. To be sure they are produced through human authors and reflect the culture, background and personalities of those authors. However, at the deepest level it is the sovereign almighty God who utilized that culture, that background, and that personality to communicate the exact words that He wanted to communicate both to the original audience that it was written to and to all believers until Christ returns for His church.

THE UNIQUENESS OF THE BIBLE

This chapter is not attempting to lay out a detailed apologetic for the inerrancy, preservation and authority of Scripture, but a few thoughts here are important. Other so-called "holy books" such as the Hindu Vedas, the Book of Mormon or the Qur'an cannot reasonably be compared to the Bible. The Bible stands alone both in terms of its message of the one true God who is creator and redeemer and its preservation through the centuries.

One common attack against the Bible is that even if the original manuscripts were divinely inspired or God-breathed, they have been so corrupted through the years that we cannot know with any certainly what the originals said. However the manuscript evidence for the New Testament is so much greater than any other document from antiquity that there is no comparison. For example, the Hindu Vedas, said to be originally composed as early as 1500 BC have no extant manuscripts before the eleventh century AD.[2] That is a period of well over twenty-five hundred years with no textual evidence for documents that are purported to be directly heard from the divine.

In stark contrast to that we have hundreds of New Testament manuscripts along with thousands of quotes from the New Testament within three hundred years of the original writings. Just for comparison purposes, the Greek philosopher Plato wrote in the fourth century BC and the earliest manuscript evidence we have of Plato is from the ninth century AD.[3] This is a gap of over twelve hundred years. In addition, there are seven known manuscripts of Plato's writings. Compare this to the New Testament. There are over fifty-six hundred Greek manuscripts. In addition, there are over nineteen thousand other manuscripts in the Latin, Aramaic, Coptic and Syriac languages. This is a manuscript base of over twenty-four thousand manuscripts with remarkable reliability between the manuscripts.[4] On top of this we have literally tens of thousands of quotes of biblical passages attested to by both Christian and non-Christian writers in the first few centuries after the New Testament was written. I have never heard a discussion indicating that we cannot possibly know what Plato actually wrote. How absurd is it in the light of the manuscript evidence to state such a thing about the Bible?

Muslims claim that every word of the Qur'an was a direct revelation of Allah to Muhammed spoken by the angel Gabriel. They claim that it is the only book containing God's revelation that has never been altered or corrupted throughout history.[5] The problem is that there is no textual evidence at all to corroborate such a claim. Contrary to the claims of Muslim apologists, the authority and prominence of the Qur'an in Islamic thought did not develop for several hundred years. The Qur'an itself flatly contradicts the Bible at numerous points and flatly denies the divinity of Christ, his sacrificial death and his resurrection.[6] Allah is not another way of understanding or naming the God of the Bible; he is a false god. The teaching of the Qur'an cannot be harmonized with the teachings of the Bible. They present an antithetical understanding of the person of God, the way of salvation, and the person and work of Jesus Christ.

The Bible was written by over forty human authors over a period of about 1,500 years.[7] Much of it is written as the narrative history of people that has been authenticated through archeology, writings from the Ancient Near East, and ancient non-Christian historians. The Bible routinely gives specific details of historical events and continues to hold up under intense scrutiny from the unbelieving world as the most accurate historical document of antiquity. Year after year and decade after decade, discoveries are being made which show that the Bible accurately portrays the people, places and events that are described in its pages.

On the contrary, the Book of Mormon, which supposedly lays out the history of inhabitants in the Americas from 2200 BC to 400 AD, is completely bereft of any archeological confirmation of its historical claims. There is not a single shred of evidence left behind that speak of the people and the culture referred to in the Book of Mormon. The advanced civilization of millions of people who built temples, rode chariots and worshiped Christ with Hebraic roots has not left a trace of evidence to verify the authenticity of the book's claims.[8] Flatly stated, there is no reputable archeological evidence that the contents of the Book of Mormon are true. This book, believed by Mormons to be sacred Scripture, is a fable that contains no historical truth.

The Bible is altogether different. It is God's word given to us that we might know Him. The Scriptures help us to know God accurately in all of His unique glory. Ultimately from beginning to end the Scriptures lay out in a plethora of ways the story of the great creator/redeemer who rescues his fallen creation from their well-deserved tragic end. Jesus Christ, the living Word, comes to save mankind from experiencing the eternal righteous wrath of the holy and just God by His brutal sacrifice on Golgotha's hill. He takes the sin rap for all who put their trust in Him and drinks the cup of God's wrath to its very dregs. The good news, proclaimed in the pages of the Bible, is that those who give their lives to Jesus by grace through faith, have been set free from the penalty of sin, are being set free from the power of sin and will ultimately be set free from the very presence of sin! This is the good news. And it only comes in one place—the Bible.

HOW TO CONNECT WITH CHRIST THROUGH THE BIBLE

Many people have grown discouraged with trying to understand the Bible. Recently I was in the southeastern African country of Malawi on a missions trip where we taught a basic course on systematic theology. We were overwhelmed by the response. Many of the people who attended testified that they had almost given up on reading the Bible because they could not understand it. They were confused and befuddled by it and could not make sense out of it. Many of them were believers but they had never been taught how to read or understand the Bible. They were in a cultural context where many false prophets were declaring lies and using Bible verses as their proof texts. Many people in America and throughout the world have also been so inundated with false teaching and false teachers using the Bible that their confidence in ever being able to really understand it for themselves is severely undermined.

The first thing you need to know in order to grow in your knowledge of God through the Bible is that *God wants you to know Him!* He is not playing a game with you whereby He teases you into thinking that you can know Him in a certain way and then gaining pleasure by frustrating you. God has not breathed out His word and preserved it over centuries so that you will not be able to understand it. A foundational Christian doctrine is the clarity of Scripture. This doctrine states that the ordinary reader can understand the meaning of the biblical text and therefore come to understand God more accurately through reading the Bible. Of course we understand that a heart darkened by sin does not readily believe what God reveals about Himself. A Christian, however, is equipped to understand the Bible in such a way that it will help them to grow in the knowledge of God so that they might live a life submitted to the Word of God.

This is not to say that every aspect of Scripture can be fully understood. Even Peter, inspired by the Holy Spirit, indicated that some of Paul's letters were "hard to understand" and that the "ignorant and unstable twist [them] to their own destruction, as they do the other Scriptures" (2 Pet. 3:16). These words are written in the context of Peter exhorting believers to "grow in the grace and knowledge of our Lord and Savior Jesus Christ" (3:18). Peter is saying that although there are some things that are difficult to understand, the word of God is both sufficient and clear enough for anyone who diligently reads it to grow in their knowledge of God.

There are five critical things that believers must do in order to grow in their knowledge of God through reading the Bible:

1. Read the Bible prayerfully.
2. Read the Bible contextually.
3. Read the Bible continually.
4. Read the Bible Christianly.
5. Read the Bible submissively.

First, believers must read the Bible *prayerfully*. The Bible is God's Word breathed through his Spirit and will only be rightly understood through the working of the Holy Spirit in the believer's life. This means we come to our reading of the Bible with the prayerful expectation that God wants to speak to us! He gives us His word so that we will know Him. Jesus says in

John 10:27, "My sheep hear my voice, and I know them, and they follow me." Come to the reading of the Bible expecting to hear from God.

Secondly, believers must read the Bible *contextually*. No one would take a novel, assign chapters and verses to it, and then tell someone to go to chapter 10 verse 14 and tell us what it means! Anyone would know that to understand that sentence you would need to understand the paragraph, the chapter and the whole context of the story leading up to it in order to rightly understand the impact of that sentence. The same is true with the Bible. Although chapter and verse numbers can be helpful for us, they often become a hindrance by making us think that we can understand a certain verse without understanding its context.

Growing in our ability to know God through His Word means that we should read not just isolated verses but entire books of the Bible. Because the Bible is a compilation of sixty-six books written over a 1,500 year period there are many different genres of writing (history, poetry, wisdom literature, epistles, etc.) and many different contexts (Ancient Near East, Babylonian Empire, Roman domination, etc.). A growing familiarity with these elements, which is aided most by consistent reading of the text, helps the reader to know what the author is teaching or speaking of to the original audience. When this is rightly understood the reader can then begin the process of making appropriate application to their own life. The living Word becomes alive to the reader as they rightly understand it and apply through reading it in context.

God has designed it so that coming to understand the Bible well is not a difficult task for the normal Christian. Getting a good and easy-to-read translation is important. Many people can easily invest in a good study Bible which is the most important tool you will need. My personal favorite is the ESV Study Bible, but there are many others that are good as well. Any believer who owns a car, goes on vacation or goes out to eat more than once a month definitely has the means to get a good study Bible.

Thirdly, believers are called to read God's word *continually*. If you are what you eat, it is no wonder that so many believers are spiritually anemic, powerless and confused! How many of us would say at the end of a day or a week, "Oh I guess I just forgot to eat"? We don't forget to eat because we know that we need food to live. We also don't forget to eat because we enjoy eating food. By God's grace we need to develop the same attitude toward the reading of Scripture. We must come to understand that we need it to live and that we look forward to reading it. Psalm 1:2 encourages believers to meditate on His Word day and night. This is an idiom that encourages ongoing meditation on the Word of God as the lifestyle of the believer. We must read God's Word continually.

Fourth, we must read the Bible *Christianly*. By this, I mean we must read the Bible with an understanding that Jesus is the center of the Scripture. The Old Testament, or Hebrew Bible, points forward to the coming of Christ. The New Testament points us backwards to Jesus' first coming and forward to his second coming. In Luke 24 we see the resurrected Jesus walking with two disciples on the road to Emmaus. They are distraught because Jesus was crucified but they were perplexed by reports that Jesus had been resurrected. At this point Jesus Himself gives them perhaps the greatest Bible study ever. "And beginning with Moses and all the Prophets, he interpreted to them in all the Scriptures the things concerning himself" (Luke 24:27). Jesus takes up the Hebrew Scriptures and shows them throughout the sacred writings how they testify to Him.

As believers we should always be looking at not only how the Scriptures point us to Jesus but also specifically how they show us the gospel. This is critically important. When we understand that the promises of God to Adam, Noah, Abraham, David and all of Israel culminate in one person, Jesus Christ, the Scriptures come alive to us. When we see that the message of the gospel—that Jesus Christ comes to die for our sins and set us free from its power—is foreshadowed and preached throughout the Scripture, we are encouraged and empowered to walk with God.

Fifth and finally, we must read the Bible *submissively*. An understanding of the Scripture without a commitment to obey it is a sure sign of an unconverted heart. Believers do not stand over the Bible as they read it but under the Bible as they commit themselves to worshipful obedience. Let me be clear. We all fall short in our obedience—and our salvation is not based on our obedience but on the perfect obedience of Jesus. However, when a person is born again he or she is given a new heart—what the Bible calls a "heart of flesh" as opposed to a "heart of stone" (Ezek. 36:26). Along with the new heart, God gives His Spirit to His people so that they will walk in His ways and obey His rules (Ezek. 36:27). As believers read the Scriptures they must do so with a willingness to obey the voice of Lord.

In all of these ways we read the Bible so that we get to know the character and heart of God. When I first gave my life to Christ I remember wanting to read many books about by newfound faith but somehow sensing that I should not. For my first two or three years as a believer the book I read was the Bible—over and over again. This has ended up being a great blessing in my life. Now I do believe that there are many great books that can help us grow in our love and knowledge of God, but there is only one that is indispensable. All other reading must supplement our reading of Scripture and never replace it.

It is not wrong for a new believer to read other books to supplement Bible reading, but it is important to ensure that what you are reading contains sound doctrine and will not lead you astray. The final form of the Bible that we have today is known as the "canon" of Scripture. The word canon means an accepted rule, principle, or standard of judgement.[9] The Bible stands as the final rule, standard or authority by which any doctrine must be judged. In the end, we can know that a doctrine or teaching is sound if it concurs with the truth that is revealed in the Bible. This is why it is so important for believers to read the Scripture and have a basic idea of how to interpret it. Reading God's Word becomes the great privilege of every believer that with the help of the Holy Spirit helps us to grow in faith and in the right knowledge of God.

CONCLUSION OF THE UPWARD MOVEMENT

The upward movement involves: 1) recognizing Jesus Christ as central, 2) relying on the power of the Holy Spirit and 3) submitting our lives to God's word. As we do this we are reorienting our lives towards communion with God and commitment to God. As we reorient our lives in this way we see that every aspect and element of our lives involves worship. We are commanded and empowered to build our lives around worshiping the one true God. As we commit ourselves to grow in our worship of the true God we begin to see our other affections, unattached from a proper view of Christ and His Lordship, lead us to idolatry.

Embracing the upward movement demands a radical change from relying on self or other things or people, to relying on God Himself. This requires a fundamental paradigm shift in how we understand our lives, our world and our relationship with God. Accepting the fact that God really does want us to know Him intimately means that my time and priorities must shift to make this a reality in my life. Even the good things in our lives that we once made "ultimate" things must be reconfigured to take their proper place.

I recently saw a social media post by someone who said, "I love sports, I love the Lord, and I love my family." This reflects an-all-too common way of expressing affection that does not differentiate between my love for the God who saved me and the local sports team that entertains (and frustrates) me. When I say that Jesus and mint chocolate chip ice cream are both "awesome," there is a problem. Family, politics, career, marriage, sports, food and everything else must take a back seat to pursuing relationship with Jesus. In reality we will find that each of those pursuits is changed and enhanced as they fall into their proper places. Knowing and loving Jesus makes us more effective for His glorious purpose in every relationship and pursuit. I can actually enjoy football and ice cream more because I no longer look for them to fill a gap in my life that they were never designed to fill.

As our lives become more centered on Jesus we become more and more able to understand the inner workings of our own hearts. This leads us to the second movement—the inner movement. This movement enables us to know ourselves rightly so that we grow in our ability to love God and others well.

The foundational nature of the upward movement moves us to value Jesus above all else. As we reorient our lives to connect with Jesus, this will inevitably have a massive impact on how we understand ourselves. The impact of a Jesus-centered life necessarily disrupts our "business as usual" approach to life and creates a radically different foundation for self-understanding.

Lord, I want to know You. Help me to diligently seek You in Your Word. Increase my passion to read Your Word and make me a fervent seeker of You. Enlighten the eyes of my understanding that I might know You rightly and discern between truth and error. Guide my steps by Your merciful and gracious hand. I pray all these things in the matchless name of Jesus, my savior, redeemer and Lord. Amen.

PART TWO

THE INWARD MOVEMENT

FINDING CHRIST IN THE INNER JOURNEY

If you look for truth, you may find comfort in the end; if you look for comfort you will not get either comfort or truth, only soft soap and wishful thinking to begin, and in the end, despair.

—C.S. Lewis

We have explored the idea of the upward movement of the believer as he or she marshals all of their resources to make connecting with God the priority of their life. This is the ongoing priority of the life of any believer. However, if there is to be depth in the believer's knowledge of God the second movement is essential.

It is impossible to come to know the Lord in any significant way without having to explore the intricacies of your inner world. The upward movement is always accompanied by a powerful inward journey towards true self-knowledge. In this movement our connection with Jesus unmasks the layers of lies that we have believed and held on to in order to survive the crushing blows that relentlessly come against us in a sin-soaked world. With His perfect love, God asks us to come out of the boat of our worldviews and coping mechanisms that help us make sense of life and step out onto the water of His unfathomable love.

We begin this movement in a place where we are living out our desperate attempts to control life so that we will not be wounded. Layer upon layer of lies color our every thought as we grapple for a way to think well of ourselves against the onslaught of the encroaching forces of sin from both within and without. We start in a place where the primary goal is to maintain our dignity and find meaning and purpose by any means necessary.

The goal of this movement is to bring us to a place where we have faced the very worst that this world has and we no longer have a need to control anything. We have submitted ourselves to the rigorous examination of the Great Physician and have concurred with His dread diagnosis. In doing so, however, we have found freedom and healing at the deepest level. We acknowledge that our attempts at self-salvation are hopeless and we let go of our obsession for control. This is a journey from a life dominated by gripping fear to a life lived more and more with the open hand of faith.

The end of this movement is a place soaked in the peace of God where we are no longer driven to fight to the end for our own sense of dignity. The end of this movement is the active acceptance of the work of another that secures for us what we could never secure for ourselves. Instead of fighting to find meaning and purpose for our lives, we accept the meaning and purpose that has been bestowed on us by our God. When we accept the meaning and purpose that God assigns to us we are set free by Him to truly love God and others with a whole heart.

7

CHRISTIAN IDENTITY CONFUSION

And we do not know who we are because we do not know whose we are. We have lost the awareness that we are the children of God.

—Gardner C. Taylor

"Who am I?" "Why am I here?" These are the most basic questions of life that every person faces. And every person, either unknowingly or knowingly, builds their lives around how they answer these questions. So do you.

I remember watching a documentary about the some of the problems that are routinely faced by ex-professional athletes. In our culture, athletes are awarded great praise and status and, if they are exceptional in their performance, also great wealth. The documentary explored how many of the attributes that served to make an athlete exceptional on the playing field, such as their hyper-competitive drive and their ferocious desire to be noticed, often lead to their ruin when their playing days are over. Unable to fuel the attention-addiction and the adrenaline rush that were naturally filled in their athletic careers, they find other outlets to meet these needs that often lead to both personal and financial ruin.

But what is true about some athletes on one level is true about all of us. When we build our identities on the wrong things, these things will ultimately cause our destruction. The interesting thing is that this is equally true for Christians and non-Christians. The star athlete and the star preacher face many of the exact same pitfalls. To be honest it is often easier for the preacher to deceive himself into believing that those pitfalls are not really there. For the preacher, and any other Christian for that matter, to derive their primary identity from their performance and the benefits that come from "doing well" is a recipe for disaster. The inward movement helps us to connect the reality of what we have learned about God with the reality of our own souls. Growth in a Christ-centered life demands that we throw out every understanding of self that is not based in the truth of Scripture and an honest assessment of the state of our souls.

Knowledge of self, if it is to be helpful in conforming us to Christ's image, must be rooted and grounded in a holistic understanding of what the Scripture has to say about us. I am afraid that too often Christians opt for a truncated understanding of self that serves to simplify things and give us a straightforward way of understanding ourselves and our world. Very seldom, however, does such an uncomplicated view serve to move us forward in conformity to Christ. To the contrary, such simplifications make faith in Christ much more complicated!

DEVELOPING FALSE IDENTITIES

There are two main issues that Christians routinely run into when developing their identities. The first is the view that highlights that we are sinners. We will call this the depravity-centric view. Those in this camp are ready to repeat the words of Jeremiah 17:9 in any and every circumstance: "The heart is deceitful above all things, and desperately sick; who can understand it?"

Those in this camp often operate as if the descriptions of mankind given in Genesis 1 and 2 don't exist. There is no room for a primary understanding of human beings as image bearers of God. The dignity of humanity, and the glory of the plan of God, is forfeited due to the lack of scriptural emphasis on the original creation and the exalted purpose that God has for human beings now. They even miss the promise of Ezekiel 36:26 that promises to remove the old, stony heart and give believers a new heart that can be molded by God.

For the depravity-centric camp our sinful state becomes the byword through which we can understand all we need to know about ourselves particularly and humanity as a whole. "All have sinned and fall short of the glory of God" (Rom. 3:23). "There is none good, not even one" (3:12; Ps. 14:3; 53:3). In the depravity-centric camp we may add the fact that we are saved by grace, but most often this is seen as something that has a lot more significance after we die than it does right now. Failure is expected and our sinful Jeremiah 17:9 hearts are to blame (along with Satan and the world, of course). For goodness sake, even the great apostle Paul seemed discouraged beyond measure regarding his own ability to walk with God in those famous verses from Romans 7:18–20.

> For I know that nothing good dwells in me, that is, in my flesh. For I have the desire to do what is right, but not the ability to carry it out. For I do not do the good I want, but the evil I do not want is what I keep on doing. Now if I do what I do not want, it is no longer I who do it, but sin that dwells within me.

We spoke in the last chapter about a correct interpretation of Romans 7, but for those who are depravity-centric a wrong understanding of this passage adds fuel to their fire.

For those who live in the depravity-centric camp their sinfulness is very likely to become an idol. Like any idol, it becomes the thing around which life is built and the rubric through which the world can be rightly understood. My depravity replaces Christ as the center of my thoughts and understanding. I bow to the power of this idol every time I fail to obey Christ's commands. Now here is the powerful part—I quickly go to receive the comfort that the depravity-centric idol offers me. Since my heart is corrupted my sinful failings are inevitable. Comfort. This is not only true of me but of everyone else as well. Comfort. God would really be wrong to expect anything else because He either made me this way or at least allows me to continue to be this way. *Ahhh . . . sweet comfort.*

And so this idol does what every other idol does—it leads me away from Christ and comforts me with lies about the nature of God, myself and the world. And in the end submission to this idol produces weak, ineffective and bedraggled believers at best, and graceless, hopeless pseudo-Christians at worst. As with all other idols, what once promised comfort leads to confusion and chaos. I am left in a far country, estranged from the only one who is able to heal, save and deliver me.

The second school of thought highlights that fact that we are new creations who are born again and made in the image and likeness of Christ. We are new creations (see 2 Cor. 5:17), more than conquerors (see Rom. 8:37) and able to do all things through Christ (see Phil. 4:13). Furthermore we have died to sin and have been set free from it (see Rom. 6:2, 7). Christ is at work in us to do His "perfect" will (see Rom. 12:2). Although these truths are important points of emphasis in Scripture, they are taken out of context and not understood properly. Instead of becoming truly Christ-centered, this view becomes fixated on an ideal that refuses to acknowledge the reality of sins present power at work in us. In practice this denies what Scripture clearly declares—that we are in desperate need of Christ every minute of every hour of every day. We will call this camp romanticized-believism.

According to romanticized-believism, the sinful nature has been dealt with to the degree that it is no longer a major issue for true believers. There are some theological systems that are centered on this. However, I am less concerned with systematic theology supporting this view than I am with the casual portrayal of this type of truth in much modern preaching and teaching. Essentially our innate goodness just needs to be properly encouraged and activated to set us on a course that eclipses one degree of glory after another.

I remember taking a seminary class with a brother who was strongly in this camp. When a professor was speaking about our need to repent daily because we often fall in sin, my classmate strongly rebuked the professor in the middle of the class. He said, "Ye do err, not knowing the Scriptures or the power of God" (quoting Matthew 22:29 from the King James Version). Stuck on an exalted view of self that was based on a wrong understanding of Scripture, he quickly made himself the teacher and defied anyone to come against him.

Romanticized-believism also has the capacity to become a powerful and self-intoxicating idol. Effective idols and lies almost always contain a substantial core of truth. The word of God with a twist is used in tempting both Adam and Jesus to sin (see Gen. 3; Matt. 4). In Matthew, as a matter of fact, Satan uses the exact words of Scripture to tempt Jesus (see 4:6). Can you imagine the audacity of the Evil One who uses the words of God against the One who is the Word of God? The words, however, are pulled out of context and used wrongly and with evil intent. Although all of the things quoted above regarding romanticized-believism are true in and of themselves, they are ripped from Scripture in such a way that their understanding is twisted.

The effective idolatry of this camp is to inflate our understanding of self and effectively dismiss our urgent, ever-present need for Christ. To maintain this idolatry I must lie to myself about the incredible pressure that sin constantly puts on me and my consistent failure to honor God with a whole heart. I either dismiss my need to repent or I repent in superficial ways. In my sin I find the comfort of an idol that tells me that my sin was merely a mistake or an anomaly. Comfort. That it is not really me and besides, real sinners do things much worse! Comfort. My unrestrained thoughts are not really sin because I did not act them out. Comfort. Even though I hurt others deeply because of my actions, God knows my heart (i.e. my clear, good, and godly intentions). *Ahhhhh . . . sweet comfort*!

Self-knowledge that leads us to a Christ-centered life understands and embraces the dynamic tension that Scripture unswervingly adheres to. Believers are sinners and believers are saints. Believers are new creations freed from the power of sin and lowly creatures who struggle and fail and sin every day. Believers are radically new creations but not totally new creations.[1] Glory, tragedy and grace live as intimate neighbors in the daily life of a believer and we are never far from any of them. Image bearers of God, fallen creatures, redeemed sons and daughters, helpless and dumb sheep—each of these describes every person who believes in Christ. We are not simply one or the other, but we are both and all. Self-knowledge that serves to transform us centers upon one irreplaceable reality—in believing we have been made one with Christ.

UNION WITH CHRIST

When I was in high school I was a big fan of Bruce Springsteen and Billy Joel. I did not sing, perform or play an instrument. I had never seen either of them in a concert. I had no musical talent to speak of. And yet when I look back at my high school yearbook I see that many of my friends saw this connection between myself and two guys I had never met. Why?

It must have been because I talked about them so much. I cannot really remember now but I must have let people know over and over again how much I loved an album or a song that described something that I was feeling. When people thought about me they thought about Bruce and Billy. My zeal for their music insured that people who knew me at all could not help but know how I felt about these artists. I was a big fan and part of my identity was tied to my fervent identification with these artists. It would be impossible to know me for long without knowing about Billy and Bruce.

Admittedly this is a very weak analogy for what the union of a believer with Jesus Christ is like. There are some parallels, however. For the believer, union with Christ becomes their primary functional identity. Union with Christ is not merely a snapshot or perspective that describes the life of a Christian, it is the essential reality that both makes one a believer and insures ongoing life-transformation. It is impossible to know a Christian on any deep level and not know that they have a deep love and commitment to Jesus Christ. By the way, if you are reading this and you believe that people can know you well and not know this about you, you may want to reconsider where you really are in relationship to God. If people consistently know more about your favorite sports teams or music preferences than about your love for Jesus Christ then something is radically wrong.

Too often when we think of knowledge of self we consider feelings, circumstances, family histories and temperaments without first and foremost rooting our understanding in what God has to say about who we are. As believers, the overriding reality of our identity is this—we are in Christ! Jesus has died for me specifically and I have been crucified with Him (see Gal. 2:20; Rom. 6:3). Not only that, but He has been raised to new life and I have been raised with Him (6:4). Who I am is radically and profoundly tied to who Jesus is. To know me apart from knowing about Christ would be like trying to describe what I look like without using my body in the description. It is impossible.

When believers understand that union with Christ is their primary identity, they avoid the traps that those in the depravity-centric and romanticized-believism camps fall into. This understanding gives life Christ-centered purpose and power that we are meant to possess. It highlights the grace of God because we are aware of how drastically unworthy we are of this. We can sing along with all of His redeemed:

> My sin, oh, the bliss of this glorious thought!
> My sin, not in part but the whole,
> Is nailed to the cross, and I bear it no more,
> Praise the Lord, praise the Lord, O my soul![2]

We glory in the finished work of Christ to forgive and cleanse us of sin but at the same time we acknowledge our ongoing struggle with sin. We do this, however, centered in Jesus Christ.

DEVELOPING A PROPER IDENTITY

The central struggle for Christians is developing a proper identity. I have struggled most of my life with centering my identity on the wrong things. As a pastor it is easy to equate ministry performance or church health with my identity. When things seem to be going well I'm good, but when they go badly I am in trouble. The truth of the matter is that the greater issue, from God's perspective, is my attitude when things go well. I no longer see my urgent need for the work of Holy Spirit in my life every waking hour.

Christians often build their identities on sinking sand. For many who have struggled through great difficulties in life and have received counseling for it, their identities can be built on their diagnosis. Years ago a close friend who I dearly loved struggled with this. His psychological diagnosis had become the primary determining factor in how he understood himself and his ability to work through difficult issues. This became particularly evident in times of high stress. He had been taught this through years of interaction with well-meaning counselors. The problem is that this had undercut his ability to bridge the gap between his formal theology and his functional theology. Regardless of his ability to articulate Christian doctrine in a theological conversation, what kicked in when he faced difficult struggles was a functional theology with an identity built around his psychological diagnosis.

This is extremely common for believers and it takes on many forms. For those with addictions and life-besetting sins, it is easy to form their identities around these things while living under a patchwork of Bible verse Band-Aids that substitute for a Christ-centered identity. On the other hand, many successful and highly productive people fall into the same pit but it is often undetected because it is dressed up so nicely. Identity becomes centered on the accoutrements and trappings of "success." And it looks really good. The problem is that positive outcomes, material trappings, the respect of others and a highly regarded reputation have subtly pushed Jesus Christ out of His rightful place. And He will not have it!

Identity built on anything but Jesus Christ is a trap. If my identity is built around my sins and struggles—this is death. If my identity is built on my successes and accomplishments—this is death. If my identity is built on my perfect kids, perfect marriage or perfect reputation—this is death (and also a big fat lie that will soon be exposed). Christ is my life (see Col. 3:4). In Him I live and move and have my being (see Acts 17:28). All things hold together in Him (see Col. 1:17). Sins and successes fluctuate like the tides, but Jesus Christ is the same yesterday, today and forever (see Heb. 13:8). In reality the only sure and lasting thing that I can hold onto is Jesus Christ.

In the inward movement we grow towards a more Christ-centered life when we build our identity properly on union with Him. I used to think that a right understanding of God helped me achieve a "good balance" in my understanding of myself as both sinner and saint. I am now convinced that God is not looking for "balance" at all. I am not being accurate if I try to balance my understanding of myself as a sinner and a saint by downgrading the full weightiness of either of these. The truth is that any downgrading of my sin condition (i.e. "I'm not THAT bad") leads me away from a lifestyle of radical dependence on the grace and power of God. To downgrade my calling as a saint has a similar affect. "After all," I may reason, "God knows I'm human." This demonic logic is often the thought that precedes a precarious fall into sin that is made possible by mitigating my calling and status as a saint [Greek *hagios*: holy one].

Embracing the full depth of the sinner-saint condition causes me to run with a whole heart to Jesus Christ. Recognizing the overwhelming reality of my need for Christ, I realize that I cannot trust in anything or anyone else—least of all myself. Acknowledging the weight of my saintly calling in light of my fleshly lust for sin I realize that Jesus is my only hope.

It is against this backdrop that all the other things I hold onto for identity begin to fade away. My sin is covered and swallowed up by the gospel. My accomplishments and victories are never mine alone but are a gift to me from my amazing Savior. Jesus, who is my all-in-all in reality, becomes my all-in-all in my daily thought process. My heart cherishes Him as never before and my hands cling to the only one who can save me.

NECESSARY STEPS

This second movement, the inward movement, requires that believers embrace at least three things in order to truly grow in such a way that Jesus becomes the center of our lives. The following things are required:

1. A radical commitment to honesty about where we are finding our identity.

Winston Churchill once famously described Russia as a "riddle wrapped in a mystery inside an enigma."[3] Although I'm not entirely sure what that means I think it is a good description for the identity of any believer who does not have his or her identity wrapped up in Christ! Confusion. Having been brought to new life in Christ we are nonetheless inconsistent and imperfect in our devotion to Him. Whenever we tie our identity to our performance we are in trouble, and yet if we are honest we do this often.

I have struggled with viewing myself honestly for most of my life. After being married for a few years, I remember my wife saying, "You don't love me like you think you do!" *Ouch . . . that hurt*! I hated her words, but they were true. My love for her was more about how I derived benefits from her than about benefits that I gave to her. Until I became honest about my lack of genuine love, I would not grow in love. This is the pattern in every area of our lives. Embracing the real truth about ourselves is the first step to actually knowing ourselves rightly in relationship to God.

2. A gospel-based understanding of how I am viewed by God.

Christians suffer from ongoing identity confusion because they do not recognize and accept at a deep level, how they are viewed by God. When I become preoccupied with how I am viewed by others, I have already lost the battle. The beginning of developing an identity based on union with Jesus Christ is recognizing all the other things in my life that I am currently leaning on to develop my identity. Anything or anyone from whom I derive my primary source of self-understanding apart from their proper relation to Jesus Christ has become an idol to me. In the depravity-centric model we discussed above there is an unproductive and ungodly preoccupation with my own sin. In the romanticized-believism model there is an unhealthy and prideful view of self that diminishes both my sin and the holiness of God.

Although you might now see yourself as belonging to either of these camps you should take some time to consider which one you may lean toward. In my experience most believers lean toward one model or the other to shield themselves from dealing with the effects of their sin. In fact it is very possible to lean toward one camp sometimes and the other camp at other times. For example, I may employ the self-help strategy of romanticized-believism at a point when my sin is a secret from others and pretending that all is well makes me feel better. Once I my sin is exposed I may run to the depravity-centric model which enables me to lump others in with myself and not feel the full impact of the weight of my sin. In each case I shield myself from coming to grips with full effect of my sin. At the same time, I miss out on experiencing the wonder and power of God that only comes when I deal honestly with God about where I am really at. What are some ways that you typically shield yourself from the awful truth about your sin? How might things look different for you if you were to rightly apply the gospel in that situation?

It is only in the gospel-based understanding of myself that I see three critical components come into alignment: My sin is worse than I ever imagined; my God is holier than I ever thought; and God's grace is more powerful, persistent, and penetrating than I could ever have possibly hoped for. Instead of putting up my hands to shield myself from the guilt of my sin and the wrath of God, I stand behind Jesus who has died in my place already for that very sin. My freedom comes as I embrace the truth of my identity through the lens of the gospel.

3. Embracing humility.

There is no room for a proud heart in the presence of God. Making Jesus the center of my life means that I am living my life in conscious awareness of the presence of God. This means that Jesus is not over there somewhere—He is here! The reality of my sin and the greater reality of His love and grace lead me—like Moses, Isaiah and Paul—to glory in Him alone and find no confidence in my flesh. I embrace a position of humility that allows me to be honest about my own sin and forsake my attempts to take a little bit of God's glory for myself.

Let me make this really practical. As I write these pages I have been the husband of Harriette for over three decades. It is not wrong for me to acknowledge that being her husband is a part of my identity. However, this must not stand on its own. My identity as a husband is tied to Christ. I am called to "love her as Christ loved the church and gave himself up for her" (Eph. 5:25). Ultimately my identity as a husband is to love my wife in such a way that the mystery of Christ's love for the church is revealed by the way I love her (see 5:32). Therefore my "husbandly" identity does not stand by itself, but stands in and under my relationship with Christ. This same logic is true for every area of our lives be it as parents, students, employees, or business owners. It is the grid through which we view our race, ethnicity, national or regional affiliation and even our family of origin. *Everything!* Everything must be filtered through the grid of our relationship to Jesus in order to rightly configure our identity.

God's glory is magnified through our lives as we embrace the incredible reality of our need for Jesus at every level. I am now, and always will be, dependent on Him for everything. Living in purpose-filled dependence frees me to see myself more accurately in relationship to the only One who loves me perfectly. In the next chapter we will explore what this looks like in more detail.

Lord, I am Yours,
Everything I have, everything I desire,
and everything I love belongs to You and finds it
value in You.
Lord, help me to lift my eyes to You alone,
Not to define myself by things which are here today
and gone tomorrow.

Help me Jesus, to cling tightly to You,
And to value those things that
are dear to Your heart,
That I might build my identity in You,
To the praise and glory of Your name. Amen.

8

THREE ELEMENTS OF A CHRIST-CENTERED IDENTITY

Jesus came to announce to us that an identity based on success, popularity and power is a false identity—an illusion! Loudly and clearly he says: "You are not what the world makes you; but you are children of God."

—Henri J. M. Nouwen

Congruity. Logic. Simplicity. I find great peace in these concepts. When I feel like I really understand something then there is a confidence and comfort that I have that is otherwise lacking. And, according to a Christian worldview, this is one of my major problems. Let me explain.

I remember encountering a doctrine in seminary that I had never heard of before. It was called the "simplicity of God." "Wow," I thought, "this should be really helpful." Herman Bavinck, the great Dutch theologian described it this way: "Simplicity here is the antonym of 'compounded.' If God is composed of parts, like a body, or composed of genus (class) and differentiae (attributes of different species belonging to the same genus), substance and accidents, matter and form, potentiality and actuality, essence and existence, then his perfection, oneness, independence and immutability cannot be maintained."[1] In essence what this doctrine means is that God is simple in that

He is perfect in everything He is. He is perfect in His holiness. Simple. He is perfect in His justice. Simple. He is perfect in His love. Simple. He is perfect in His mercy. Simple. The heart of this doctrine is the understanding that God does not merely have attributes of love, holiness and justice, but that God *is* love, justice and holiness. God is a perfect integrated whole and not a set of competing parts or attributes that can be ranked in order of their importance.

There is, however, an issue with all this simplicity. How these things actually fit together is anything but simple for us to understand. I understand that God is perfectly just—but it is hard to reconcile, in my finite mind, that He is also perfect in mercy. His perfect justice demands my death for my sins, but His perfect mercy sets me free from death and gives me eternal life based on the merits of Jesus Christ and His substitutionary death on my behalf. Now, I like this because it obviously works in my favor but simple is not the name that I would give it!

The point is that the peace that I often find in things being simple can often become an idol in my life that leads to shallow thinking and therefore shallow faith. This becomes a major issue working against my Christian growth when in the name of simplicity I neglect to pursue the uncomfortable, difficult and often seemingly contradictory truths that are critical in the formation of Christian identity. It is one thing to say that my identity is found solely in Christ, but quite another to actually live out of a Christ-centered identity.

Living out of a Christ-centered identity demands that my identity accurately reflects how I am seen by God. There are at least three essential ideas that make up our identity in Christ that need to be fully established if we are to see any real progress in dislodging false identities and become truly grounded in Christ. The ideas are these: 1) I am a beloved child of God, 2) I am a sheep desperately in need of help and 3) I am a person who is being conformed to the image of Jesus Christ. Although these may seem to conflict with each other, it is important to establish and develop each of these elements in order to actually build our identity around Jesus Christ. If any one of these elements is left out, our Christ-centered identity will be lopsided and compromised. We will always miss out on the true riches when we opt for that which is neat, logical and comfortable. Growth in Christlikeness is none of these!

I AM A BELOVED CHILD OF GOD

The first essential idea of identity is based entirely upon what God Himself has said and done. It is true that Christian conversion demands a response of faith and repentance, but as one growing in Christ I am loath to take credit for these things. When I was spiritually dead it was God who opened my eyes to my sin (see Eph. 2:1–3). It was God who gave me a new heart that cared about what He said and desired to follow Him (see Ezek. 36:28–32). It was God who made me a new person by joining me to the life of Jesus (see Eph. 2:4–5). I understand that the new person that I am as a beloved child of God is a result of His work both for me (in the cross of Christ) and in me (by the renewing power of the Holy Spirit—see Titus 3:4–7).

For this work I deserve no credit because it is totally a work of God's grace (see Eph. 2:10). By definition, grace is the unearned and unmerited favor of God. *Grace is the "just because" goodness of God applied to His beloved but fallen creatures.* The believer who is growing in Christ cries out, "Why me?" not as one accusing God, but as one who is overcome by His mercy and grace. From a worldly perspective I understand that there is no good reason why God should choose me of all people. I am blown away by His extravagant mercy and humbled by His redeeming love for me.

And all of this mercy, this astonishing love of God, leaves me in the place of accepting the new identity which God gives—***I am His beloved child***. I have been adopted into the family of God and now possess all the rights and privileges of sonship.[2] "The Spirit himself bears witness with our spirit that we are children of God, and if children, then heirs—heirs of God and fellow heirs with Christ, provided we suffer with him in order that we may also be glorified with him" (Rom. 8:16–17). That actually means what it says—as God's children we get full shares in the inheritance that was earned by Christ! Though we did not earn it, this glorious inheritance is credited to our account based on the finished work of Jesus.

If this is all true, and it is, how is it that as believers we so easily get caught up in our day-to-day reality that we totally lose the perspective that is afforded to us as children of God? We are in a brutal battle to keep the eyes of our hearts stayed on the reality of our new identity. We have demonic forces all around us and fleshly forces at work within us frantically pulling us to a perspective that will not recognize the new and eternal reality that exists for us as God's beloved children. This is where the practices outlined in chapter 3 become so important. If we don't become people who stop to be with God often, and who meditate deeply on what He has done for us, we will quickly loose our perspective and see very little real transformation in our lives.

Do you meditate often on your identity as a child of God? Is that identity growing more and more real to you on a consistent basis? Now you need to be really honest as you answer these questions. What is your primary identity, really? Is it in your work, in your marital status, in your family of origin (for good or bad), or in your economic status? Is it in your title, your job description, your reputation or your passions and hobbies? Unless your self-understanding as a child of God crushes all these others in terms of importance, your transformation in Christ will be shallow at best. Your work is to establish a primary identity that has nothing to do with your natural origin, your gift and talents, or your standing and reputation. Your work is to establish your primary identity based on what Jesus Christ has done for you. For the believer in Christ this means one thing—my primary identity is simply—***Child of God!***

I AM A HELPLESS SHEEP

Having established this we go on to the second essential idea of identity: ***I am a sheep desperately in need of help***. This strikes the balance that is missed in the two camps we talked about in the last chapter (the depravity-centric and romanticized-believism camps). Having acknowledged my new status as a child of God whose sins have been washed away by the finished work of Christ, I now look into a clean mirror in a bright room and see all the flaws, imperfections and sins that still cling to every part of my being. If I am even the least bit honest about my thoughts, intentions and actions, no one who knows what I know about me would confuse me with being Jesus!

Sheep are helpless animals with no real defense against an attacker. Because sheep are easily led and have an instinct to flock together, they have been domesticated throughout human history. Most sheep have only one real defense that they can be confident in—their shepherd. Apart from the shepherd who is there to lead them and keep them safe, sheep have no way of overcoming an attacking predator.

Just as a sheep is no match for a pack of hungry coyotes, so the believer is no match for demonic forces, worldly allurements or fleshly lusts. Each of these powers is more than sufficient to take down a believer and lead them to ruin. It is interesting that sheep have such a strong instinct to follow that they will follow a leader even to their own ruin. If the lead sheep were to walk off of a cliff and perish, all the other sheep are likely to do exactly the same thing. It is not an overstatement to see how much like sheep we are in this respect. Even when we pride ourselves on our independent thinking, we are likely being drawn by the same ungodly passions that have led many others to destruction. Because we do it "our way" we think that we are unique and special. But such pride is really nothing new at all. It is Lucifer demanding to be worshiped (see Isa. 14:12–15)[3] and Adam and Eve following his lead by demanding to "be like God" (see Gen. 3:1–8). The seminal instinct of sin is to make oneself the center of things and thus dethrone God.

And so believers must understand themselves as sheep. Although we pride ourselves on our intelligence and our ability to determine our own path, in truth we are being led by someone else. *The question is not whether you are being led but by whom you are being led.* To embrace our "sheepyness" is a countercultural act of humility. In a day and age where "branding" is not only for products and companies, but for individual self-promotion, believers are all branded with one mark as sheep. Deeply embracing this facet of identity often goes against modern Christian culture but it finds good company in Jesus' words from the Beatitudes (see Matt. 5:3–12).

It is no wonder that Scripture points to Jesus as the Good Shepherd (see John 10:11). In Psalm 23 the Lord, Yahweh, the one true God of Israel, is pictured as a shepherd. It is because He is the shepherd that David can say, "I shall not be in want" (Psalm 23:1—translation mine). True security and peace can only come when the Lord is our shepherd. The sheep is safe when the Good Shepherd leads. The sheep is protected when he stays in sight of the Good Shepherd. The sheep is provided for when he follows the direction of the Good Shepherd. Biblical "shalom," deep and abiding peace, soundness and well-being, is the result of the believer consciously and consistently yielding themselves to the care of the Good Shepherd.

Any sheep fending for him-or herself is simply a lamb chop in waiting! It is just a matter of time until they become some lucky coyote's lunch. The same is true of a believer who forgets their desperate need for Christ. I need Him. Now. Desperately. Every second of every minute of every hour of every day—my desperate need is to be strongly tethered to Jesus Christ. My identity as a sheep ensures that I don't forget for a second who I am and who I am not. I am not able on my own to protect, to produce or to provide for myself or anyone else.

It is this true sense of ongoing desperate need that insures that believers exhibit genuine humility. Tragically, humility seems to be one biblical virtue that has been relegated to the sidelines in many modern day evangelical circles. It has been deemed as relatively unimportant especially if someone is particularly gifted. The cult of worldly stardom, fueled by the need for recognition, has crept into the church. When this happens someone other than Jesus becomes the main attraction.[4] Transformed believers are marked not so much by their giftedness as by their humility.

Even those who are greatly gifted are constantly pointing not to themselves but to Jesus.

What is it about us that resists understanding ourselves as sheep? The same "I can do it myself" mentality that we hear from a toddler who insists on tying their own shoes, persists throughout our lives. There is something that rises up in us that would rather die than be pitied. I remember a few years ago being in a therapeutic group with several other pastors. We were talking with one particular brother and, according to the prescribed process, taking turns in giving our insights based on things that we had noticed. While I was in the middle of what I thought was a "deep" insight, one of the leaders interrupted me and indicated that my point was irrelevant and unhelpful. I was angry. Furious. Everything in me wanted to lash and out and choke him because I felt that I had been disrespected in front of this group of men.

My anger was fueled by my intense desire to be seen as someone with wisdom and helpful insight. At that moment clearly this was about my glory and not God's. My rage revealed to me just how much I resisted and resented being a sheep. As much as I would love to teach and proclaim how "sheepy" I was, I was not ready to live in the reality of "sheepyness." The sheep humbly looks to the shepherd and does not take up arms to defend himself. Self-aggrandizing pride is swallowed up by a constant gaze upon the shepherd who alone becomes the hope for my provision, my protection and my right position in His kingdom. My identity is swallowed up in the shepherd and does not demand to be noticed and admired by anyone.

I AM A GLORY REFLECTOR

Understanding myself as both a child of God and as a helpless sheep in desperate need, I now come to the final point of self-understanding. I understand myself as ***a person in the process of being conformed to the image of Jesus Christ***. As such, I was made to powerfully reflect God's glory in the world. This essential idea of self-understanding is indispensable if one is to recognize their identity as being rooted and grounded in Jesus Christ.

The Bible lays out for us the purposes and plans of God from the beginning to the end. The first two chapters of Genesis lay out the glory of God's purpose in creation which is highlighted by one particular creature who is said to be made in the "image and likeness" of God himself. Of course that creature is man, both male and female. While every element in creation highlights some aspect of God's majestic greatness, it is mankind particularly that was created to show off His glory in high definition. Adam and Eve were to benevolently rule over and care for God's creation as His vice-regents. This is precisely why the fall of Genesis 3 is so overwhelmingly tragic—the creature that fell into sin was the closest thing to God Himself in all of creation.[5] This creature committed high treason against His creator and declared his independence from the one who both created and sustained him. You and I do the same thing every time we sin.

And for this reason the Christian life cannot be understood merely as declaration of who we are by God's grace (children of God) or by our ongoing desperate need of Him (as sheep). It must also include the element of God's transforming power presently at work in our lives. The work that God began in creation moves always toward its fulfillment. That fulfillment is described in many ways in Scripture. Isaiah 11:9 describes it this way, "for the earth shall be full of the knowledge of the Lord as the waters cover the sea." Revelation describes a scene as the consummation draws near:

> After this I looked, and behold, a great multitude that no one could number, from every nation, from all tribes and peoples and languages, standing before the throne and before the Lamb, clothed in white robes, with palm branches in their hands, and crying out with a loud voice, 'Salvation belongs to our God who sits on the throne, and to the Lamb!' (Rev. 7:9–10).

The primary product of time is the redemption of a people for God's glorious purpose. The Lord describes Himself as a bridegroom awaiting His bride. "Let us rejoice and exult and give him the glory, for the marriage of the Lamb has come, and his Bride has made herself ready; it was granted her to clothe herself with fine linen, bright and pure—for the fine linen is the righteous deeds of the saints" (19:7–8). God's glory is greatly magnified as those who were dead in their sins, without hope and without God in this world and fully committed to their own way, are displayed as trophies of His wonderful, powerful, life-transforming grace.

This reality demands that the identity of the believer be grounded in the idea that they are in a process of transformation that is directed by God Himself. They are, to use Jeremiah's terminology, on the wheel of the potter. It is God alone who has the right to determine the use of the clay, and He will mold it to His own liking. The good news for the believer is that God has made His sovereign design known. Believers in Christ are those whose lives are being progressively molded into conformity with the image of Jesus (see Rom. 8:29). No circumstance, no difficulty, no tragedy, and no seemingly random interruption to life holds any power to determine ultimate direction. God alone is all-powerful. He is the potter who has destined to make those who believe in Christ vessels of eternal worth and value. He is going after every flaw and imperfection in the clay and every imperfect element in its structural design in order to remake for Himself a worthy vessel. Like the earthly potter He will push, cut, squash and continually remake the clay until it looks like what He originally intended for it to be. His will *will* be done!

This is incredibly good news for the believer. It is through this grid that believes must view all of life. My family of origin is not an accident or a mistake. The sin perpetrated against me does not have the last word on my identity. My own sinful actions and ongoing tendencies and addictive patterns do not define me and will not conquer me. As this reality sinks deeply into my soul I can give up my idol of control and rest my life in the hands of Jesus even as the clay sits in the hands of the potter.

And so we are called to answer the most basic questions of life that we asked at the beginning of the last chapter:

Q: Who am I?

A: I am a Christian, a child of God, a sheep under the care of the Good Shepherd, and a person being radically transformed to be like Jesus.

Q: Why do I exist?

A: I exist so that every part of my life will bring glory to Jesus Christ. I have been created by Him, redeemed by Him and look forward to an eternity of unspeakable joy in worship and service to Him.

Are you seeing your life more and more in these terms? Not just when you are reading a book, praying, or in a Bible study but when you are bored and lonely on a Friday night? When you are overwhelmed with work and school and a to-do list that is running you ragged? When our identity is being formed by our relationship to Jesus, our present circumstances no longer dictate our core identity.

BEING SET FREE FROM SIN

Transformation into the image of Christ means that God is at work in you to destroy the grip of sin on your life. His glory is displayed as sinful patterns and behaviors are overcome by His power at work in your life. As we have discussed earlier in chapter 4, it is not possible to be born again of the Spirit of God and not be progressively transformed to talk more, walk more and live more like Jesus. Sin is acknowledged, confessed, repented of and gradually overcome in the life of God's children.

John's first epistle masterfully lays out this truth. He is writing to the church in Ephesus (modern-day western Turkey) in the later part of the first century. Ephesus was a city full of false gods, idol worship, and competing ideologies. The false teachers he is confronting minimize sin and even change the definition of it in order to say that they are without sin. In response John writes:

> If we say we have fellowship with him while we walk in darkness, we lie and do not practice the truth. But if we walk in the light, as he is in the light, we have fellowship with one another, and the blood of Jesus his Son cleanses us from all sin. If we say we have no sin, we deceive ourselves, and the truth is not in us. If we confess our sins, he is faithful and just to forgive us our

> sins and to cleanse us from all unrighteousness. If we say we have not sinned, we make him a liar, and his word is not in us. (1 John 1:6–10)

Verses 6 and 7 make it clear that the way that a believer lives is distinct. The first truth is this: God calls His children to live righteous lives. He calls this "walking in the light" and contrasts it with "walking in darkness." Christians are those, He says, whose lives are marked by walking according to the light.

The second truth is this: God calls us to a life of continual confession of our sin. At first blush, the second truth seems to be in direct contrast with the first, but we will see how it is not. Walking in the light demands that believers are continually made aware of any ways in which their lives are deviating from God's righteous path. The false teachers that John is confronting shamelessly changed the boundary markers on what God called sin so that they could claim to be without sin in their lives. God says they are liars! Christians never need to justify themselves by minimizing their sin. When we embrace God's view of our sin we can run to the One who has justified us by His perfect sacrifice for our sins. The blood of Jesus is sufficient both to "forgive us our sins" and to "cleanse us from all unrighteousness" (1:9).

Our Christ-centered identity is not compelled by worldly swagger but by God-glorifying dependence on Jesus. It is not my "can do" attitude that gives me props, but a "He did" attitude that makes little of self and much of God. By God's grace, the deep need to build an identity for the purpose of propping up my name dies so that I might spend my life and energy in building up His name.

Now we know that prideful and arrogant attitudes do not die easily. Though they may die many deaths they seem to have great resurrection power! That power is the unrelenting call of the flesh, the sinful nature, to make much of self. And this is the ongoing sanctifying work of God in the life of every one of His children—dying over and over again to our flesh that we might live more completely for God.

Establishing these three elements of a Christ-centered identity is critical for ongoing meaningful growth in Jesus. As beloved children we are grateful to the One who has adopted us into His family. As needy sheep we are dependent on the Great Shepherd who provides for us in every way. As those being conformed to the image of Jesus we live in gratitude and awe at the ongoing work of God in our lives. As these three images are held together we have a proper sense of identity in Christ. This identity empowers us to relate to God in ways that bring Him glory and to others in ways that promote life. Stripping ourselves of every false identity we glory in God as we are properly clothed in the righteousness of Jesus Christ.

SEEKING HALO FERTILIZER

I spent much time in my early years as a believer looking for the key that would allow me to reach a state where sin would no longer be a constant struggle in my life. I guess in some ways I was looking for some halo fertilizer that would insure me a place among the holy and righteous ones. I might as well have been searching for the fountain of youth! We grow older and we struggle with sin, these are two indisputable facts in the life of every honest believer. All of the miracle creams, plastic surgeries and injections in the world do not reverse the fact that our bodies are getting older and ligaments, tendons, muscles, bones and organs are wearing out. Your body has an expiration date and you cannot change it.

This is not to say that under the providence of God we do not have the obligation to do our best to care for our bodies. Indeed a lifestyle including proper exercise, adequate rest and eating healthy foods is likely to lead to a longer life. Of course, if you get run over by a bus it does not matter if there was celery and asparagus in your system or Twinkies and Snickers bars. Ultimately the length of our days is determined by God.Lord Jesus, You know that I have looked for life apart from You. I have found my identity in many things, making much of them and little of You. Forgive me, Lord, for my idolatry. Quicken me today by Your Holy Spirit every time I try to forge my identity from something that is not You.

Be glorified in my life as I look to You as my only true source of life and the One in whom and through whom is the substance of all things. Strengthen me, Lord, in all of these things, that Jesus may be clearly seen through my life. I ask all these things in the name of Jesus, to whom alone be all glory and honor and praise. Amen.

9

BECOMING A SERIAL REPENTER

One of the reasons why revival tarries is that Christians don't repent—no one wants to talk about sin.

—Eric Mason

I was an eighteen-year-old freshman in college. I was raised in a religious home and considered myself a Christian. I hoped I would go to heaven and thought that I probably would. My hope was based largely upon my self-made mathematical equation that saw my sin as not really being all that bad. I was a pretty good guy in my estimation and certainly not as bad as some others I knew. On the whole I was thinking that God would probably be making a wise decision if he let a nice guy like me into his heaven.

What a mess! Shortly after going to college I began to get letters from my best friend Kevin who had gone into the Air Force. A man who bunked next to him in boot camp attempted suicide. It was a bloody, startling and life-changing event for my friend. Kevin turned to Jesus, and in his letters to me he spoke of his newfound faith. I was confused and all of this seemed weird to me.

Providentially I had two roommates in my dorm room. My first roommate, Sam, was like me in many ways although he was a much better athlete and a young man with rugged good looks (me not so much!). He was also very religious, but that was pretty much a Sunday morning thing. Saturday night, and the rest of the week, belonged to him. My other roommate, Darryl, was different than any person I had ever met. Darryl read his Bible—often! On several occasions I came into the room and he was on his knees praying. On a Wednesday night he got back late to the dorm room and he told me he had been at prayer service. On a Wednesday night! I didn't have any precedent for seeing someone with this type of devotion to God. I was confused.

I admired Darryl and saw a peace and calm in his life that I wanted to have. I saw Sam's lifestyle of partying and carousing with women and something deep inside of me knew that it was wrong and I should not give myself to it. I did anyway. I was away from home and had freedom to experience life for the first time without restraints. I failed miserably. I fell miserably. I sinned fervently.

But God was at work. He used Kevin and Darryl during that time to show me, for the first time in my life, the depth of my own sin. They were not berating me about it, but they were simply loving God and walking with Him. Through them, I saw my weakness and my hopelessness for the first time. The equation that always had me slipping into heaven to do God a favor no longer worked. I came to crisis and all my old answers failed. I didn't need to "get better" (I couldn't)—I needed a savior! Thanks be to God through Jesus Christ that during this time I discovered the wonder of the reality that there was true life offered through relationship with Him. This was way beyond my religious worldview where I hoped I did enough good to outweigh the bad. I came to grips with the wretchedness of my sin and in doing so for the first time I saw the greatness of Jesus Christ as Savior.

Many believers can offer a similar testimony regarding how they were awakened to the reality of their sin and their need for Christ. Moving from a religious experience to a deep dependency on Jesus is a common theme for many Christians. The mysterious working of the Holy Spirit convicts me of my sin and points me to the need for a relationship with Jesus through repentance and faith. These are the necessary seeds for introduction to the family of God. Only in acknowledging the depth of my sin am I prepared for new birth as a child of God.

THE TRUTH OF THE STRUGGLE

Sadly, this initial experience is often singled out as something that is unlike the rest of the Christian life. "Come as you are" is the unqualified call to the unconverted. This includes the idea of coming with your sin and mess and the promise that Jesus will forgive and cleanse you. However, the message to veteran believers is often something very different. Saintly credentials are quickly called into question if someone should make known their present sin failures. Somehow it's okay to say I struggle with pride, but some other sin issues (particularly of a sexual nature) quickly call my conversion into question. And so many Christians live like our first parents after they sinned in the garden. Life becomes about living with a series of fig leaves to cover up our true selves and play a life of hide-and-seek in "Christian" community.

The gospel frees us up to be honest about who we are and about our deepest struggles and failures with sin. Christians do not need to downplay sin or call it something else because Jesus died for our sins (not mistakes, habits, addictions or mental health issues). Honest talk about real sin issues and how the gospel engages our ongoing struggles and failures with sin can be our catalyst to Christ-centeredness. God is using everything in your life to bring you closer to Him—even your sin! This is a necessary implication of Romans 8:28. Included in the "all things" that work together for the good of believers is their own struggles and failings with sin.

SEEKING HALO FERTILIZER

I spent much time in my early years as a believer looking for the key that would allow me to reach a state where sin would no longer be a constant struggle in my life. I guess in some ways I was looking for some halo fertilizer that would insure me a place among the holy and righteous ones. I might as well have been searching for the fountain of youth! We grow older and we struggle with sin, these are two indisputable facts in the life of every honest believer. All of the miracle creams, plastic surgeries and injections in the world do not reverse the fact that our bodies are getting older and ligaments, tendons, muscles, bones and organs are wearing out. Your body has an expiration date and you cannot change it.

This is not to say that under the providence of God we do not have the obligation to do our best to care for our bodies. Indeed a lifestyle including proper exercise, adequate rest and eating healthy foods is likely to lead to a longer life. Of course, if you get run over by a bus it does not matter if there was celery and asparagus in your system or Twinkies and Snickers bars. Ultimately the length of our days is determined by God.

Every believer will struggle with sin every day of their life until they go to be with Jesus. What that struggle looks like will be very different, however, based on how we exercise the spiritual muscles God has given us, how we learn to rest in Him, and what our daily diet from this world and from God looks like. Spiritual exercise, spiritual and physical rest and a healthy spiritual diet create a much greater likelihood of more consistent victory in our struggle with sin. However, such a lifestyle, which brings us into closer communion with God, also allows us to see levels and depths of sin that we otherwise would never pay attention to. The reality is that those who have experienced the greatest degree of outward transformation live with a greater awareness of their present struggle with sin and their need to consistently repent for failing God. They are serial repenters.

WALKING IN THE LIGHT

This is exactly what John is getting at in First John 1:5–10. According to John believers are those who "walk in the light" (1:7). John says that those who walk in darkness "do not have fellowship" with God. The interesting thing that John says here is that that those who walk in the light are cleansed from their sin by the blood of Jesus. Walking in the light does not mean that a person is without sin. It cannot mean this because verse 8 clearly states that "if we say we have no sin we deceive ourselves, and the truth is not in us." The one who walks in light actually sees his sin so that he can confess it and repent of it!

The beauty of the gospel is that we do not have to hide for fear of God, but we run to Him as our hope and our redeemer! Looking honestly at our sin is not a hopeless life of introspection that leads shame and guilt. Much the opposite. It is a life of freedom and hope inextricably bound to the finished work of Christ. True repentance brings deep and abiding joy.

Jesus was an anomaly to the religious leaders of his day. He consistently broke their traditions and did things in a way that did not fit the mold of a prophet. Though the miracle power working through Him was undeniable, there were several factors that called into question the source of His power. Jesus' disregard for the Sabbath, His continual association with tax collectors and sinners and His lack of reverence for the traditions of the elders were consistent issues that the Pharisees and Sadduces had with His ministry. Furthermore, the ongoing buzz was that He claimed to be the Messiah and possibly even God's son.

Although the atmosphere in Palestine was ripe with Messianic expectation, there was very little about Jesus that seemed to fit with that expectation. They were looking for freedom from their Roman oppressors, and yet He seemed to have no such interest. In fact, instead of challenging Caesar He seemed to save His harshest words for the Jewish religious elite. Surely this disqualified Him from having the status of a prophet, let alone of the expected Messiah.

GOOD NEWS TO THE WRONG PEOPLE

The radical message of Jesus was good news to the wrong people. He was "a friend of sinners" (Matt. 11:19) and this was not an appropriate title for any so called prophet. He surrounded Himself with uneducated and crude men. He ministered to and associated closely with women who had questionable backgrounds. He consistently took the side of known sinners when they were confronted by more righteous people. Their conclusion was that His power was demonic. His clear stance on the side of the worst people gave them great clarity on this fact.

But the accusation of the first-century Pharisees was what made the gospel good news to the first-century sinner. Two thousand years of history have done nothing to marginalize or diminish that good news. Jesus' mission statement in Luke 19:10 made to Zacchaeus is that exact same to us today, "For the Son of Man came to seek and to save the lost."

When we as modern day believers understand this truth, we are able to bring our sin into the light and no longer make it something other than what it is. Every believer is confronted with a critical choice that will dramatically affect the timing and manner in which they are being conformed to Christ's image. Will I make my life about seeking fertilizer for my halo or will I become a serial repenter? There is really no middle ground, although believers often will go back and forth between the two.

THE CHOICE OF REPENTANCE

Seeking halo fertilizer makes my holiness the starting point of my journey. Becoming a serial repenter makes Jesus' holiness the starting point of my journey. Seeking halo fertilizer means that I intrinsically possess what I need to make God satisfied and I am simply seeking a few sprinkles to go on top of my elegant and well-frosted cake. Becoming a serial repenter means that I consistently see the ugliness of my sin and my need to throw myself at the feet of the cross and plead for mercy. I am not a well-frosted cake in need of a few sprinkles. As a matter of fact, if my identity is in Christ I no longer see myself as the cake at all!

All attempts at bolstering self-esteem and self-worth apart from our connection with Jesus are doomed to fail. I do not need to talk about how good or wonderful I am, but I am focused on how good and wonderful Jesus is. I also understand that by His unfathomable grace He has loved me and called me to be His child. For believers, self-esteem is never based on self apart from connection with Jesus. The basis for self-worth and value is that I have been created in the image of God and redeemed by His Son for the purpose of giving Him glory in both time and eternity.

Serial repenters live in close communion with others and tell on themselves all the time. Repentance is a regular practice for them and those who are close to them see it. Their spouse sees it. Their kids see it. Their coworkers see it. If they are a pastor their congregation sees it. They are growing in the ability to come out of hiding with their sin and are learning not to go into a defensive posture when their sin is exposed. They are learning the freedom of living before God and not merely before men. They are learning to value God's redeeming love above the praise of men.

The last several years of my life have been more full of repentance than any other time. Is it because I am now sinning more than I ever have before? I certainly hope not and I don't think so. It is because I am more aware of my sin than ever before and more willing to quickly repent. Whether that is to my wife or children, to my fellow pastors at my church, to someone from the congregation, or just to God. A healthy grip on the gospel allows us to come out of hiding, stop blame-shifting and confess our sin.

SELF-PRESERVATION OR DEATH?

Years ago I had a neighbor who had spent much of his early life in combat in both Korea and Vietnam. I remember many long conversations with Mr. Dave in my neighborhood. I was blessed to have him as a neighbor as he would constantly look out for everyone on the block and help me with projects around my house. One thing that Mr. Dave would always land on was this saying: "Self-preservation is the first law of nature." His thinking was conditioned through his experience of war and by the many battles that he fought to see life in this way. I could relate and I could understand, but the Bible would not allow me to agree.

Jesus is the king of clarity. He did not urge us to self-preservation but to dying to self. "For whoever would save his life will lose it, but whoever loses his life for my sake will find it" (Matt. 16:25). These famous words of Jesus come to us in a very interesting context. Earlier in this chapter He had asked His disciples to tell Him what people were saying about Him. He got all the standard reports. Some said He was John the Baptist. Some said He was Elijah and others said He was one of the prophets. But then He asked the truly important question, "But who do you say that I am?" (16:15). At this point Peter steps up and makes his great confession of Holy Spirit-inspired faith, "You are the Christ, the Son of the living God" (16:16).

Jesus commends him for this statement and tells him that this was revealed to him by the Holy Spirit. Jesus then begins to talk to his disciples about the fact that He is about to suffer, die and be raised from the dead. Peter reacts saying, "Far be it from you Lord! This shall never happen to you!" (16:22). Jesus responds by saying to Peter, "Get behind me Satan! You are a hindrance to me. For you are not setting your mind on the things of God, but on the things of man" (Matt. 16: 23).

Within a few short verses Jesus goes from telling Peter that he has heard from the Holy Spirit to identifying him with Satan himself! Wow! This is the immediate context of Jesus statement in verse 25 that indicates our need to willingly lose life in order to find life. A life of repentance is a life that embraces death to self. Serial repenters do not fight for their dignity or position but willingly admit to their corruption. Serial repenters do not find some way to preserve "self," but understand that the only self that matters is the one that has been united with Christ. "Set your minds on the things above, not on things that are on earth. For you have died, and your life is hidden with Christ in God" (Col. 3:2–3).

The inner journey that causes us to know Christ intimately is filled with a million deaths. The everyday and all-the-time pleadings of our flesh must meet with a response. When we fall in deed, word or thought the Holy Spirit faithfully convicts us of our sin. This brings us to the point of decision that moves us to spiritual union/life or spiritual estrangement/death. Our first parents, Adam and Eve, chose the way of cover up which always leads to estrangement and death. Because of this, the impetus to cover up is in our fleshly DNA. Our flesh is hard-wired to take the path that will pull out every stop to preserve our dignity at all costs and make us look good. God shows us another way.

THE WAY OF CONFESSION

The way of confession—clear, complete and without excuse—is the pathway to life. Such confession followed by repentance means the death of everything "self" that is not unified with Christ. It also means the infusion of Spirit-filled life to the believing believer. The inward movement is radically attached to and informed by the upward movement and enables the believer to consistently find life in the midst of death. Growth in Christ necessarily means that we see ourselves more and more accurately through God's eyes. We see ourselves to be more flawed, corrupted and wicked than we had ever imagined. We see ourselves to be more loved, empowered and cared for than we could ever hope for. And this 20/20 vision fuels a growing single-minded desire to crown Jesus Christ as Lord of every area of our hearts.

And so Christians are called over and over again to decide between confession and cover-up. If you are not living out of a secure place of gospel-centered/Christ-centered awareness you will choose cover-up every time! It is not by clinging to self that you will ever find life but by losing every part of self that wants recognition, strokes and glory that is not connected to Jesus. Settled relationship with God through the finished work of Christ and the ongoing power of the Holy Spirit allows you to honestly confront sin though a lifestyle of confession and repentance and therefore to make real progress in overcoming sin in your life.

There are several elements of confession that we should be aware of. Our tendency to confess and yet save self is very real. Frequently I will hear semi-confession that go something like this, "I am very sorry if I may have hurt anyone by something that I might have done." Instead of being a real confession this is actually a self-saving mechanism that is not specific and subtly blames the victim for their thin skin.

The practice of confession should include at least five elements:

1. **Confession is frequent.** When you understand that you have sinned and/or hurt someone it is time to confess. If you are growing closer to Jesus this will happen with increasing frequency.
2. **Confession is specific.** Confession is never a mea culpa that takes ownership for a general sense of something going

wrong. Confession conveys specific information about what was done in a wrong, sinful, and hurtful way.

3. **Confession is personal.** Confession does not downgrade the degree of my wrongdoing by talking about the culpability of others. When I confess I focus on how I have sinned and take full responsibility for that.
4. **Confession is nondefensive.** The posture of confession is not to save self but to die to self. Therefore the one who is confessing can hear from others about their hurt with empathy toward them and a willingness to embrace an even deeper level of accountability.
5. **Confession is tied to repentance.** The biblical ideal of confession is always closely tied to repentance. Confession is not a self-serving exercise to get something off of my chest. It is done, prayerfully in the conscious awareness of God's presence, as a part of turning away from sin and toward God. Without the element of repentance, confession is merely a psychological or religious exercise with no eternal value.

Serial repenters are people whose lives are on a trajectory of knowing God with increasing intimacy. They have realized once and for all that as beloved children and bedraggled sheep they do not have to "make it happen" for themselves. They can find rest, true rest, in the arms of the One who knows every dark secret and every wandering thought, but has chosen out of eternal and omnipotent love to adopt them into His own family. Therefore they have found that a lifestyle of ongoing repentance leads to a life of rest and thankful gratitude. Covered by the blood of Jesus there is no need for any other thing to make me appear acceptable. Christ has done it—it is finished!

O Lord, help me to walk in Your light,
Let me cast away the life of darkness
and shadows,
Where I have hidden from myself, from others and
from You.

I thank you, Lord, that You did not turn away from
me in my sin,
But You turned toward me.
You loved me.
You lived, You died and You were resurrected for me.

I therefore gladly will confess my sin to You,
And pray for deep and true repentance.
For everything in me that is not from you has died,
And my life is now hidden in Christ.

Thank you, Lord, for Your overwhelming love,
That I, even I, would be a vessel of Your glory.
May You be ever glorified through my life.
I pray these things in the name of Jesus,
My savior, my redeemer and my Lord. Amen.

PART THREE

THE OUTWARD MOVEMENT

FINDING CHRIST IN HIS BODY AND HIS WORLD

I have learned to kiss the waves that have
thrown me against the Rock of Ages.

—Charles Spurgeon

Growing in the knowledge of God and of ourselves moves us to invest our lives deeply in the lives of others. Because we have been made in the image and likeness of the Trinitarian God, the God who eternally exists in relationship, we are both created and redeemed to live in deep relationships with others. In this third movement we will explore the two defining marks that necessarily identify how growing Christians relate to others. We will see how the essence of God as Trinity indelibly marks His special creation and sets an uncompromised trajectory of intimate involvement with others on every level.

CHRISTIAN COMMUNITY

The first defining mark for the outward movement of believers is life in the Christian community. Life lived in close proximity to other believers with the intentional pursuit of knowing and being known as well as caring and being cared for is necessary for the healthy growth of believers. Contrary to much of the modern "me-centered" existential philosophy that wraps itself in Christian garb, the Bible knows nothing of growing in Christlikeness outside of the believing community. In fact this type of mind-set, prevalent even among regular church attenders who do not commit on a deep level to Christian community, shows us just how far afield our individualistic mind-set is from God's design.

The primary soil for both measuring and enhancing growth is Christian community. It is in the community of believers, with all of their issues, problems and sin patterns, that we "work out [our] salvation with fear and trembling" (Phil. 2:13). Apart from life in the community, growth will always be stunted and measuring real spiritual growth will be impossible.

THE EVANGELISTIC CALL

The second defining mark for believers is the evangelistic call. Stated simply, it is impossible to know God deeply and not share the truth of Jesus with those who do not know Him. Believers who are growing in Christlikeness are compelled by their conviction that Christ is the only way to know God and the only means by which anyone will escape the punishment of eternal separation from God in hell. The certitude of this knowledge compels growing believers to look for every opportunity to share the love of God in Christ with those who are otherwise perishing.

Very often our conception of what it means to be mature in Christ lacks the component of consistently sharing Christ with others. *Victory* over certain areas of sin, a knowledge of the contents of the Bible, and consistent involvement in spiritual or church activities tend to be the criteria in many circles to define the *mature believer*. Notoriously lacking from this is a lifestyle that routinely shares the good news of Jesus Christ with those who are lost. If Christians actually believe that life and death are intrinsically connected to knowing Jesus Christ then the moniker of *mature* should not be handed out to those who do not make a practice of sharing Christ with others.

Being certified in CPR and having a deep understanding of the biological issues involved in resuscitation does not make me a good friend if I simply choose to impress others with my knowledge while my friend lies on the floor dying. In fact having the knowledge and yet failing to take action makes me a significantly worse friend then if I never had the knowledge in the first place!

This outward movement compels growing believers to live in community and to share Christ with others. In many ways this communal aspect of the Christian walk is what either validates or nullifies the spiritual experience that someone may speak of having in the first two movements. Authentic relationship with God and deepening knowledge of self will find fitting expression in the community of believers and in the world that Christ came to save.

10

LOVING CHRISTIAN COMMUNITY

The Bible tells us to love our neighbors, and also to love our enemies; probably because they are generally the same people.

—G.K. Chesterton

I was reeling from the sting and hurt and betrayal that I experienced in my church. It is hard to explain the depth of the hurt when it comes from the very place that is supposed to both protect you and help you to connect with God on a deeper level. Nevertheless the unchecked and unrepented-of sin of the leaders created a culture of slavish servitude that undercut any redeeming quality that could be extracted from the sermons or teaching. My twin temptations were to understand this as a betrayal by God himself and/or to see this as indicative of the church as a whole. If I took the first option it gave me a "right" to hold onto bitterness and anger against God and to punish Him by retreating from Him. In the second option I would be justified in retreating from any attempt at deep and authentic relationship in the church and to develop my personal relationship with God outside of Christian community.

Holding onto the first option would certainly lead to spiritual death—and I knew it. The second option, however, promised a form a spiritual life without the hardship, difficulties and messiness of relationships. This promised a wonderful "Jesus and me" relationship that would be unencumbered by the rules and cultures of ecclesiastical structures. This seemed to offer me a freedom to come to know Christ without anything or anyone else getting in the way. Having been hurt deeply in the context of the church (several times, actually) this was not simply a vague or light temptation. To the contrary, it seemed to make real sense to my crushed and grieving heart.

Perhaps you have experienced something similar. The two places in life where you are more or less guaranteed to experience a deep level of hurt are in your family and in the church (if you are deeply committed and building authentic relationships). The reason for this is simple. Where there is a growing depth of love between flawed human beings who struggle with sin and live in a fallen creation, we will inevitably hurt one another. This can be the result of a simple misunderstanding or miscommunication, or through neglect, selfishness or the inevitable effect of one person's sin on another's well-being. The consequences involve frustration, hurt and pain and are a part of any relationship that is growing in love. And the strange but true reality is this—the deeper the love and commitment are, the deeper the hurt and pain are likely to be.

Ultimately any decision about how I live my life as a believer must be in submission to God's Word. The fairy tale of "me and Jesus" Christianity quickly falls beneath the weight of God's Word. We will see that the Bible is extremely clear that it is impossible to grow in a deep love for God without growing in love with His people. A life not strongly intertwined in Christian community as a first priority, is strong evidence that a person has not progressed very far in sanctification. What may seem as an otherwise robust spiritual life is revealed as pitifully weak when deep and abiding relationships with other strong believers is not a critical priority.

THE CALL TO "ONE ANOTHER"

The New Testament lists at least forty citations in which Christians are commanded to interact with "one another" in order to cause mutual growth in the body of Christ. Some examples are as follows:

- Love one another (1 Thess. 4:9; 2 Thess. 1:3; 1 Peter 1:22; 1 John 3:11, 23; 4:7, 12; 2 John 5).
- Live in harmony with one another (Rom. 12:10; 15:5).
- Bear one another's burdens (Gal. 6:2).
- Serve one another (5:13).
- Submit to one another (Eph. 5:21).
- Confess your sins to one another (James 5:16).
- Pray for one another (5:16).
- Show hospitality to one another (1 Pet. 4:9).
- Clothe yourselves with humility toward one another (5:5).
- Encourage one another (1 Thess. 4:18; 5:11).

These commands are intensely practical and obviously impossible to do outside of a life lived in vital connection to other believers. The idea that I can do it on my own apart from others is based directly upon the lie that was first seen in Genesis chapter 3.

Adam and Eve were created in an environment of beautiful communion with God and with one another. They were created to be dependent upon God and to have a healthy interdependence on one another to carry out God's will in the earth. The temptation of eating from the Tree of the Knowledge of Good and Evil was the temptation to *radical independence*. We have seen earlier that it was the temptation to not need God anymore. The consequence, however, not only took on the vertical dimension of cutting off relationship with God, but it also included the dimension of broken relationship between Adam and Eve. Adam and Eve, who in Genesis 2:25 are described as being "naked and not ashamed" now begin to hide from one another and from God. In addition we also see each of them respond to God by blameshifting. Adam blames Eve and God—"The woman whom you gave to be with me, she gave me fruit of the tree, and I ate" (3:12). Eve also immediately resorts to blameshifting by blaming the serpent for her willful action.

This is so important for us to grasp because we see here the seeds of relational alienation that have been sown since the fall of mankind into sin. *Radical independence is only asserted and acted upon when I believe that I am both central and sufficient.* Being central means that I no longer need to answer to anyone. Satan's temptation was that "you will be like God" (3:5). In this temptation being like God means that I no longer answer to God or anyone else—in fact others must now answer to me! Being sufficient means that I have what it takes to make it on my own and no longer need help—not even from God Himself.

I have often seen this pattern at work in my own sin. When I justify my "little sins" or forsake God's ordained means of dealing with sin (confession and repentance), I am in effect saying, "I can do it myself." Like a three-year-old who wants to tie his shoes but does not have the adequate fine motor skills to do it, I profess my ability to do something on my own and forsake my need to depend upon God. The consequences of this are much more serious than a badly tied shoe. My sin, growing in the fertile soil of my pride, will sooner or later lead to catastrophic results. The resulting fallout inevitably touches many lives, not just my own.

THE CALL TO INTERDEPENDENCE

The assertion of radical independence cuts directly against both the nature of the Trinitarian God and His purpose for His created image bearers. Although we can say that God Himself in His unity has the attribute of complete independence and thus sovereignty, we would not assert that truth of any of the three persons of the Godhead with respect to one another. There is in fact a mutual interdependence that is exercised within the three persons of the Trinity. Clearly we have an example of the Son's submission to the Father's will as he grapples with the horror of the cross in his human condition. Father, Son and Spirit are each presented as active participants in both creation and redemption and yet have distinct roles. There is perfect unity and dependence upon one another which is then demonstrated in the relationship of mankind living in submission to and harmony with God before the introduction of sin.

This is the two-part ideal that Scripture sets forth for mankind:

1. Walking in intimate relationship with God and submission to His will.
2. Living in a community where we are known by others on a deep level.

We know that the fall of our first parents into sin radically destroyed the God-ordained harmony that existed before their sin. However, we need to be just as aware that the totality of Scripture is aimed at demonstrating God's unflinching commitment to the full restoration of relationships on both the vertical and horizontal levels. Furthermore, we must realize that this agenda is not something that God wants us to merely know a little about here and wait for its full realization when Christ comes back, but it is His "right now" agenda for His church.

CONSUMERS OR DISCIPLES?

Jesus Christ is at work now as the Redeemer/Restorer. Salvation is not limited to restoring a right relationship between God and mankind. Salvation also includes making unity, harmony, shalom and love the distinguishing marks of Christian community. Theoretically this sounds nice to most people—but there is a catch. This is not something that gets worked out in a community of people who are all consistently walking in the power and filling of the Holy Spirit. This is worked out in the messy reality of sinner/saints who alternate between real love and selfish ambition (people like me and you). Just as any successful marriage requires that both parties learn to forgive the offenses of the other, so life in Christian community demands the same.

This type of commitment has become even rarer in an age of consumer Christianity. We have been meticulously trained by our culture to shop for that which pleases us in a specific and unique way. And once we find that item we are free to discard it and look for another as soon as it no longer suits our fancy.

Consumerism may be understandable when it comes to pants, pajamas or plumbing fixtures but it is does not work in the kingdom of God. Making Christ central and growing in

His image and likeness demands that my priority of preference must change. By definition, consumers can choose according to their liking. Disciples have no such choice. Discipleship/sanctification is the process that challenges every selfish inclination to choose according to my preference.

The way of discipleship, taking up my cross and dying to self, means consistently choosing things that do not promote my comfort or ease. Discipleship means choosing those things that honor God and bless others even when it costs me much. We must never come to God or His church as consumers. There is no place for "consciples" in the kingdom!

Consistently making those kinds of decisions in an environment where I know that this will be reciprocated by others would still be very difficult—but that is not the environment that I live in. In the community of "sometimey saints" (of which I am one!) the odds are stacked against others "doing the Christ-like thing"—even if I do. This does not diminish God's demand.

THE NECESSITY OF COMMITMENT

It is impossible to measure commitment in ideal conditions because under ideal conditions commitment is not needed. It is in the messy reality of actual Christian community that commitment is tested and sanctification is produced. Perhaps no one has ever expressed this more powerfully than the German pastor and martyr Dietrich Bonhoeffer.

> Innumerable times a whole Christian community has broken down because it had sprung from a wish dream. The serious Christian, set down for the first time in a Christian community, is likely to bring with him a very definite idea of what Christian life together should be

> and to try to realize it. *But God's grace speedily shatters such dreams* . . . By sheer grace, God will not permit us to live even for a brief period in a dream world. He does not abandon us to those rapturous experiences and lofty moods that come over us like a dream . . . Only that fellowship which faces such disillusionment, with all its unhappy and ugly aspects, begins to be what it should be in God's sight, begins to grasp in faith the promise that is given to it . . . *He who loves his dream of community more than the Christian community itself becomes a destroyer of the latter, even though his personal intentions may be ever so honest and earnest and sacrificial.*[1]

The present community of believers is not set in heavenly perfection but in earthly process! Bonhoeffer insists that it is the embracing of the reality of that community, with all its warts, flaws and sins, which enables us to contribute to it and grow within it.

Making Christ central in your life necessarily entails living in a community of imperfect believers who are radically committed to one another even though they will deeply hurt one another at times. This type of community can only be realized where the gospel is being grasped and the Holy Spirit is powerfully shaping the community in grace and forgiveness. In this community, confession of sin and repentance does not become a means of control or manipulation, but an opportunity to experience grace and rejoicing. Despite the fact that this is often lived out inconsistently, there is a willingness to persevere in this flawed community fueled by the sure hope of the unflawed God who dwells within it. Sustained growth can only occur when the plant remains in the same soil for an extended period of time. Likewise the community of believers grows together through sustained commitment to one another despite their imperfections.

REPLACING "ME" WITH "WE"

In American culture we are very tempted to see our spiritual growth in a very individualistic way. Even if we acknowledge the need for community we can still see community primarily in terms of its ability to help me grow—emphasis on ME! In a culture with a cultic attraction to celebrities and stars, we can set our minds on becoming the superstar Christian who upholds the virtues and morals of the faith so as to become the great example to others of how to "do Christianity." This mode of thinking is insidiously anti-Christian and is a primary reason for the shipwreck of so many believers' lives, particularly for pastors.

This is not to say that believers do not set their minds and hearts on growing in Christ and more consistently honoring Him in word, deed and thought. Being more like Christ is always the goal. However, this must not be confused with our somehow gaining a celebrity status. In the Christ-centered life there is only room for one superstar and it is not you!

SHALLOW ROOTS AND DEEP CONNECTIONS

Nature provides and incredible illustration for understanding the power of Christian community. Giant sequoia trees can grow to 250 to 300 feet tall (as high as a twenty-five story building).[2] They can weigh up to twelve million pounds (as much as an ocean going freighter). In spite of their enormous weight their roots are not deep at all. In fact unlike most other trees they do not have a tap root that goes deep in the ground to stabilize the tree.[3] Instead the roots spread out and become intertwined in a network with all the other giant sequoia trees around them. Because of this, giant sequoia trees are never found in isolation but only in groves with other trees. Their roots can spread out to over two hundred feet in every direction and cover an area of four acres. Many of these trees are over one thousand years old and some are over twenty-five hundred years old.[4] The oldest known giant sequoia is estimated to be over thirty-two hundred years old.[5]

How do these huge trees resist the elements over centuries and even millennia to reach such great ages? It is certainly not the depth of their individual root systems—they are actually quite shallow. One critical secret to their amazing longevity is the interconnectedness of the root system. No tree can claim to be strong by itself, but they are made incredibly strong by their shared root system which allows each tree to multiply its strength through its connection with the other trees in the grove.

It is not hard to see the connection here to Christian community. Apart from our deep connection with others we do not have what it takes to resist the Enemy of our souls and live. It is our proximity to and participation in Christian community that buttresses our position and allows us to stand strong even in the midst of the most difficult storms of life. Together, as a community of believers, we overcome the Enemy's devices in such a way that Christ is greatly glorified. And in this, Jesus Christ alone is worshiped and glorified.

EMBRACING CONFLICT

There is another aspect of the giant sequoia that sheds light on how Christian community works. In order for these trees to continue to grow they require periodic fires in their groves to remove the underbrush which competes for their water supply and crowds out the seedlings necessary to produce new trees. Now it seems ridiculous to say that huge trees require periodic fires in order for them to grow and reproduce. When we think of fire we always see it as the thing that destroys the forest. However, this is not necessarily true with giant sequoias. They are equipped with incredibly thick bark, up to three feet thick at the base of the tree, which helps them to resist the effects of the fire.[6] This has worked over the centuries to produce groves of healthy trees that reproduce other healthy trees, not in spite of, but because of the effects of the purging fires!

What an analogy for Christian community! Healthy community is dependent upon periodic purging fires. Any community on earth that exists over time without significant conflict is at best not really growing and more likely is not even Christian. I have been married for thirty years to my amazing wife, Harriette. She has a deep love for Jesus and for me. Our growth together, however, has not been one of simply moving from glory to glory. The reality is that there have purging fires of conflict as we have each had to deal with our sin and selfishness and the effect that that's had on our relationship. Growth in our willingness to repent more quickly and to forgive more completely has helped us to grow together over the years. Conflict has actually served the process of dealing with our sin and helping us to grow together to be more like Jesus.

LIVING WITH FALSE PEACE

I am very afraid when I hear of a couple that does not have some serious conflict from time to time. The same goes for Christian community. It likely means that they have built in structures to keep a false peace. False peace[7] means there is a commitment to live in harmony based on a fear of dealing with unpleasant truth that may cause uncomfortable disruptions. Living consistently in false peace is incompatible with a life of faith. One reason I know this so well is because I spent many years avoiding conflict and thus stunting my own growth in Christ. Faith enables us to go into the ugly places of our own souls and in our relationships based on the redeeming power of our God to make all things new. Are you threatened by every little spark in your world or are you growing the kind of bark that allows purging fire to have a healthy effect on your life in Christ?

Can you see the necessity of the embracing the truths about yourself in the second movement that allow for healthy community? Unless you embrace a Christ-centered identity which allows you to confess and repent without blameshifting, you will not bring health into the community. Any healthy community needs a core group of people with well-gospeled lives to set an example and provide counsel to those who are struggling. Without that dynamic, communities quickly settle for false peace in a way that minimizes conflict until there is an unforeseen and disruptive explosion that usually leads to community disintegration.

How do we ensure that the fires of conflict serve the purpose of purging rather than destroying? The model that we have for this is the life of Jesus Christ himself. Jesus, unique in all the world, comes bearing the glory of God full of grace and truth (see John 1:14). Jesus does not merely reflect God's glory—He is God's glory! And in His glorious manifestation He brings the perfect fullness of both grace and truth. This is not a 50/50 mixture with diluted truth and therefore diluted grace. To the contrary, He bears truth in its 100 percent full potency with a radical commitment to never back off to make things a little more comfortable. At the same time, He brings a potency of grace unlike anything that had ever been seen or imagined. In fact the scandal of God's grace—the scandal of the cross—becomes the dividing line of both history and the fate of all humanity.

LIVING WITH GRACE AND TRUTH

The ability to deal with interpersonal conflict so that it enhances and grows community rather than destroys it, is found in a radical commitment to live out the grace/truth dynamic. Since we are not Jesus (or Holy Spirit Jr.) we are careful to do a radical inventory of ourselves (see Matt. 7:1–5), often getting input from others who will be honest with us. The controlling standard in conflict between believers is loving one another and building one another up in Christ. Because of this, "live and let live" can never be the motto for the Christian community.

Christians are called to love each other and, therefore, take the risk of engaging conflict for the sake of the other and for the glory of God. Jesus did not stop at Matthew 7:1, "Judge not that you be not judged." Rather He used this statement as an introduction for how we must rightly judge within the Christian community. After introspection there comes a moment of truth where we "take the speck out of [our] brother's eye" (Matt. 7:5). When we do not deal with issues in community we invite deep-seated bitterness and unchecked sin to become a destroying plague.

A CALL TO COMMUNITY

Hebrews 12:14 gives a twofold admonition to all believers, "Strive for peace with everyone, and for the holiness without which no one will see the Lord." In a perfect community—one without sinners—this is not a problem. However, in the community of sinner/saints that is the church, this is not easily maintained. For that reason further instruction is given. Verses 15–16 give an admonition/command to the church with three points of application:

> See to it that no one fails to obtain the grace of God; that no "root of bitterness" springs up and causes trouble, and by it many become defiled; that no one is sexually immoral or unholy like Esau, who sold his birthright for a single meal.

Unlike the pastoral epistles, Hebrews is not written to a church leader giving him instructions on how to watch over the flock. Instead it is written to believers in churches throughout Asia Minor who were gathered in many separate local church communities. The admonition at the beginning of verse 15 to "see to it" is a command for believers to mutually watch out for one another. This is not simply the job of a clergy class but to each member of the church to watch out for one another. There are three specific issues mentioned for which intervention is commanded:

1. The Centrality of Jesus
2. The Need for Healthy Confrontation
3. The Call to Holiness

THE CENTRALITY OF JESUS

First the author tells his readers to make sure that "no one fails to obtain the grace of God." In the context of the book of Hebrews this admonition would specifically be to make sure that no misses that Jesus is the center of our faith. For Jewish believers in the early church undergoing persecution, the writer of Hebrews clearly lays out the truth that everything in the Jewish Bible pointed to Jesus Christ. Jesus alone is the substance of which the Tabernacle, the sacrifices and the priesthood spoke to. The admonition here is simply this—"Don't miss Jesus!"

The Christian community must never miss this either. In every church and in most gatherings there are those who may be connected culturally or sociologically with the community, but who in truth do not know Jesus in the pardon of their sins. Rather than look the other way for the sake of "peace," the loving response is to engage them with the gospel. We do this in humility (we could be wrong) and we do this in love—but we do this! The most loving thing we can ever do for someone who is a cultural Christian is to help them see the impotence of their current condition and show them the reality of what life in Jesus Christ really is. The Christian community makes it their aim that no one within their ranks misses out on the riches of the grace of God.

THE NEED FOR HEALTHY CONFRONTATION

Second, the author admonishes his readers that no root of bitterness springs up which causes trouble and defiles many. This is a clarion call to the church to confront issues and, therefore, not allow bitterness to grow. I have experienced in my life that the greatest destroyer of community is the silent, incipid cancer of undealt-with offenses that pile up and result in poisonous, bitter and divisive factions. I have been on both sides of holding on to bitterness. When I have done this, I have felt justified in an ongoing, unloving attitude towards a brother in Christ for an offense that he was not even aware of. When I have been the victim of this, I have been shocked, frustrated and saddened that someone blindsided me by saying that they had been angry with me for years.

As believers we must faithfully confront one another so that we live in a community that promotes honest understanding, confession, repentance and reconciliation. Using the model of Matthew 18:15–20, we do not harbor resentment against others or spread stories, but speak to them directly in order to deal with the issue. The aim is reconciliation and the motive is love.

The word defile in Hebrews 12:15 literally refers to a stain.[8] In context this word speaks of moral corruption and impurity. The warning here is a very serious one for Christian community. If we refuse to confront and deal with issues in our community, the result is a "root of bitterness" which acts as a cancerous growth within the community. Bitter people beget poisonous community. The periodic brush fire of healthy confrontation avoids the overwhelming conflagration that either erupts from bitterness or continues as a slow and deadly leak which eats away at the unity of the church.

THE CALL TO HOLINESS

The third warning in verse 16 is against sexual immorality and unholiness. Apparently these are things that God takes seriously even though our culture does not. Imagine a parent allowing their three-year-old to walk out into a busy street without attempting to restrain them. We would rightly condemn this as a heinous act of neglect. We would rightly consider this to be as evil as any act of direct abuse against a child. It would demonstrate in an alarming way the total lack of love that the parent has for the child.

In the same way when the Christian community does not look after one another by admonishing one another to honor God in their conduct, we are showing a wanton disregard for life. Most often this comes about because we do not want to ruffle any feathers or be seen as some holier-than-thou fanatics. But the call to lovingly, graciously and truthfully confront our brothers and sisters (and invite them to do the same with us) is seen throughout the Scripture.

Embracing community with an expected norm of loving confrontation is extremely countercultural. In a time where the "judge not lest you be judged" paraphrase of Matthew 7:1 is the byword for "let me do me," many people in churches embrace this anti-community ethos. The reality is that every one of us will be judged for our actions—even believers. For Christians that judgment is not to determine our eternal destiny because Jesus has already paid the cost for our sins. It will, however, determine our degree of eternal reward (see 1 Cor. 3:12–15). My pastor, Dr. Eric Mason, often says that he would rather be judged by people now so that he won't need to be judged by God later.[9] This is the great value of a sanctifying community. We are actually helping each other to deal with our sins and issues in a way that cooperates with the work of the Holy Spirit!

PRACTICAL SUGGESTIONS

Based on all that has been said thus far about the importance of full involvement in Christian community, I want to give some basic suggestions for how to practically live this out. The first and most important deals with the attitude of the heart. No amount of outward conformity or commitment to meet with others will substitute for a heart-level commitment to allow others to know you deeply. One of the great consequences of mankind's sin in Genesis 3 was that we now engage in a lifestyle of hiding ourselves from others and forsaking authentic in relationships. Long before social media enabled us to create a "virtual self" persona, sinners and saints have worked hard at presenting a version of themselves that is more fiction than fact. Believers need to make a radical commitment to fight against that tendency which is hardwired into our flesh.

COMMITMENT TO THE LOCAL CHURCH

Christians need to enter into community on at least three levels. First, there must be a commitment to membership and ministry in the local church. Believers need to find a healthy church where Jesus is proclaimed and the Bible is taught. They must make a commitment to being disciples there. That will include serving in some capacity and giving of time, talent and treasures for the support of others. The Bible knows nothing of a person coming to a true relationship with Jesus and yet rejecting His body which is the church. To say, "I love Jesus but I have disdain for His body, the church," does not work (see Col. 1:24; 1 Cor. 12:27; Eph. 5:30).

Though there are many unhealthy and even ungodly "churches," there are also many healthy churches where Jesus Christ is worshiped and people are growing as disciples. Living with "church hurt" as a long-term excuse for not being meaningfully involved in the Christian community is a cop-out that ultimately undermines the discipleship and growth of a believer.

COMMITMENT TO A SMALL GROUP COMMUNITY

The next level of commitment is in a small group of believers. This can take many forms. At Epiphany Fellowship where I serve, we promote involvement in life groups. These groups are much more than a gathering of people that meet once a week to study the Bible. In fact, I warn leaders that these groups should never become simply another meeting that people check off of their "to do" list once it is done. The statement of purpose for these groups is as follows:

> Epiphany Fellowship life groups are small group communities of faith where the gospel is lived out intentionally. They are the place where we meet weekly for study, worship and prayer and interact daily in caring, sharing, service and recreation. Life groups are the place where we are challenged to give of ourselves to others and blessed to receive from others when we are the ones in need. Life groups are where the body of Christ becomes manifest as a living and life-giving organism in neighborhoods all over our city and region.[10]

Involvement in a life group is an expectation for membership at the church. Corporate worship and gatherings serve an important function for the church and for believers. However, such gatherings will never be enough to fulfill the Great Commission which is to make disciples. Life groups are actually communities of believers who are making a commitment to be the primary place where the "one anothers" of the New Testament are actually lived out.

My church has a mercy fund which we may use from time to time to help people with urgent needs. This fund is actually quite small, however. Over 90 percent of these types of needs are not met through a central fund budgeted through the church, but through the giving of members through our small group structure to meet the needs of those experiencing significant challenges. Whether it is helping a family with meals when they have just had a new baby or helping with a financial need due to an emergency, it is our small groups which are the front line for caring for people in the church. Our life groups are a primary place for discipleship as believers grow together in both the knowledge of God and the functional reality of what it means to live for Him in this crazy world.

TRANSPARENCY WITH ONE OR TWO OTHERS

The third layer of commitment involves growing in transparency with one or two other people. At Epiphany Fellowship we promote what we call "Gospel-Based DNA Groups." This stands for Discipleship, Nurture and Accountability. These groups are where two or three individuals of the same gender will come together on a consistent basis to help one another to grow in Christ. We have a specific methodology that we promote for these groups so that sin does not become the primary focus of the groups. The basic outline for the groups is this:[11]

Gospel-Based DNA Groups are clusters of two or three believers of the same gender who are committed to coming together regularly to grow in Christ. Most often they will come together on a weekly basis. There are three purposes and three corresponding practices that fuel their growth:

PURPOSES	PRACTICES
1. Knowing My God	Meditation on Scripture
2. Knowing My Sin	Introspection/Confession
3. Trusting My Savior	Edification/Affirmation

Details on how to get the most out of a group like this can be found in Appendix 2. The basic idea is that as we center our lives on Jesus we become honest in our relationships in order to promote an even greater love for Jesus. We never coerce or manipulate anyone to share personal things that they are not yet comfortable to share. The development of trust takes time. As trust is built we are able to share our burdens, issues and sins in a way that breaks the back of the Enemy and sets us free to love God and others well.

CONCLUSION

Healthy community is a place of habitual confession, confrontation, repentance, forgiveness and reconciliation. The unhealthy community that avoids confrontation leads to bitterness, rampant immorality and many people missing Christ altogether. There are many great resources to help individuals and communities develop norms and methodologies to promote healthy community and avoid the pitfalls of false peace.[12] In this outward movement of making Jesus Christ the center of our lives we acknowledge the depth of our need for others and also take responsibility to love others well. Such a community is not the unreal wish-dream that Bonhoffer warned against, but the imperfect yet Christward-moving gathering of the broken yet beloved. Apart from deep involvement in such a community, experiencing the life of Jesus will be short-circuited, stunted and perhaps simply reveal the lack of any true conversion to Christ in the first place.

Lord Jesus, help me to move towards Your people and not away from them. Give me the courage to make myself known and the willingness to enter into deep relationships with others. Watch over all of Your people and deepen our love for You and for one another. Grant this we pray in the mighty name of Jesus. Amen.

11

COMPELLED TO TELL: LIFE ON MISSION

Our lives begin to end the day we become silent about things that matter.

—Martin Luther King Jr.

I will never forget just how tired I felt. Alongside my older brother, a couple of friends and an interesting cast of older characters, we worked ten- to eleven-hour days packing onions and potatoes at the local factory. I was in high school and this was summer work. I was throwing around fifty-pound bags of onions most of the day and occasionally one hundred-pound bags of potatoes. On top of all this our foreman, Steve, was one nasty dude. On this day, however, Steve seemed more nasty than ever and I was not quite sure why.

The longer the day went on the nastier Steve got. He was making us run from one assignment to the next and barking out commands in an even harsher tone than normal. It was the end of a long week and as I thought we were about to wind down on a Friday afternoon his pace and anger just picked up more. I was done.

What I didn't know, however, is that Steve had an appointment after he clocked out. He had received a sentence for a crime that he had committed. The sentence dictated that after work on

Friday he report immediately to the local jail for the weekend. This went on for weeks. After a while we just braced ourselves for the inevitable mess that was Friday afternoon at the factory.

MISERY LOVES COMPANY

Steve had an unwritten commitment: "If I am miserable, you will be too!" He lived it out with great consistency and we all paid the price. He was dedicated to making his experience our experience. We did not have to go to jail for the weekend but we sure felt like we were there at work on Friday!

My wife has a saying that she often uses: "Hurting people hurt other people." Steve was no exception to the rule. Understanding this has been helpful for me in counseling and in friendships, and most often this is true. However, I have found that the flip side of this truth is not nearly as consistent.

Although hurting people, who have not dealt with their pain, routinely hurt those around them, for some reason blessed or happy people are not as consistent in blessing others. As a matter of fact, it is often the case that people who are particularly blessed are not focused on blessing others but on increasing their own blessedness quotient. I wish I could report this as one who has never been guilty but that would not be true. Sadly, as believers our unwillingness to share the gospel is an example of hoarding the blessings of God in a way that dishonors Him more than Steve's nasty attitude ever could.

GOD ON MISSION

Jesus came to save. Not just a few folks but "a multitude which no man could number" (Rev. 7:9). If you are a Christian you are no doubt thankful for the fact that Jesus came with a mission "to seek and to save the lost" (Luke 19:10). His mission was clear and

He was utterly true to His purpose. Your salvation is the result of His unrelenting, sacrificial pursuit of you. Yes it is true. If you are a disciple of Jesus it is because the almighty and omnipotent God has loved you from before the foundation of the world, has pursued you and found you in time so that you will eternally be a trophy of His grace!

The wonderful reality of Scripture is that Jesus' intentional and sacrificial life was not some kind of unexpected move of the Son that came as a surprise to the Father and the Holy Spirit. There was no moment of revelation by the Father where He was somehow caught by surprise by the incarnation and subsequent obedience, death and resurrection of Jesus. This was the eternal plan of God before the foundation of the world. The plan of salvation that was laid out and executed by God in the Old Testament pointed to the coming Messiah who would take away the sins of the world.

The Hebrew Bible is broken up into three sections: Law, Prophets and Writings. Each of these speaks plainly to the expectation of God's grand plan of salvation that happens on a global scale. Contrary to the belief of some, God's plan was never confined to the people of Israel or any other cultural, ethnic or religious group.

From the minute that sin enters the world in Genesis 3 we see that God is there to cover Adam and Eve and provide forgiveness for them. Immediately after pronouncing His righteous judgment due to their sin, the Lord covers Adam and Eve with garments of animal skins (see 3:21). This was much more than a divine fashion statement—it was a prophetic demonstration of the gospel! They had covered themselves with fig leaves but the Lord sees this as insufficient. By covering them with garments of skin, the Lord introduces the idea of the sacrificial death of another as being necessary to cover over their sin.

This concept had already been introduced in Genesis 3:16 which theologians refer to as the "protoevangellion" or the first gospel. In pronouncing judgment on the serpent, the Lord declares that the offspring of the woman "will bruise your head, but you shall bruise his heel" (3:15). In veiled but unmistakable language the Bible is telling us that the serpent will indeed strike a blow against the woman's offspring (he will bruise his heel), but that the woman's offspring will strike a deadly blow against the serpent (he will bruise his head). It is Jesus, the offspring of the woman (see Gal. 4:4), who fully destroys the serpent and sets God's people free.

When Abram is called by God in Genesis 12, the blessing pronounced upon him is that "in you all the families of the earth shall be blessed" (12:3). When God changes Abram's name in Genesis 17:5, his new name Abraham means "the father of many nations." When Israel is led by Moses out of Egyptian bondage they leave as a "mixed multitude" (Exod. 12:38) having with them many from Egypt who saw the mighty works of the LORD and chose to leave with the Israelites. Ruth, the Moabitess, becomes the great-grandmother of King David. When Isaiah prophesies of a coming servant who will save his people he says, "I will make you as a light to the nations, that my salvation may reach to the end of the earth" (Isa. 49:6). Woven into the pages of Scripture we see God's clear intention to save a multitude of people from every tribe, tongue and nation who will glorify Him throughout eternity.

The New Testament also unfolds the fulfillment of God's plan that was set before the foundation of the world. Jesus tells

His disciples that "forgiveness of sins should be proclaimed in his name to all nations, beginning in Jerusalem" (Luke 24:47). In the Great Commission laid out in Matthew 28:19–20 Jesus tells His followers to "make disciples of all nations." His actions demonstrate the radical commitment to save the lost (see Luke 19:10). Jesus comes for the very worst of sinners and therefore provokes the religious upper crust to murderous wrath (see Matt. 9:10–11; Mark 3:6). He is compelled to go to the hated Samaritans to meet a sexually immoral woman by a well so that she and many of her countrymen can experience the wonder of salvation (see John 4). He welcomes the touch of the prostitute (see Luke 7:36–39) and touches those who were considered unclean (see Matt. 8:2–3). In short, Jesus, moved by His mission to seek and save the lost, breaks decisively from religious convention in order to see the mission realized.

THE FAILING CHURCH

While Jesus consistently defies the religious norms and standards, the Bible clearly shows us that the early church often failed in this regard. It is interesting that the book of Acts records the reluctance of the first Christians to move beyond their comfort zones in sharing the gospel. While the word is being preached and many are being saved in Jerusalem there appears to be a lack of missional initiative on the part of the infant church to venture away from what is comfortable and known. It is not until full-scale persecution breaks out against the church in Acts 8 that we see believers being scattered to other regions to proclaim the gospel. It is not until God gives Peter a miraculous vision and arranges for a meeting with a Gentile Roman army officer that it even occurs to the new church that God wants to reach anyone other than Jews (see Acts 10). It takes the miraculous intervention of the Holy Spirit to move spirit-filled believers to dare to share Christ in uncomfortable places and with unfamiliar people.

MOVING OUT OF OUR COMFORT ZONES

Jesus Christ voluntarily leaves the eternal comfort of perfect communion with the Father and the Spirit to become a man so that He might save us. At the same time we often find it difficult to open our lips to tell others about Jesus. I have failed in this task too often.

I vividly recall seeing the police and ambulance lights flashing as I approached the Fortune 500 office building that I worked at on my way back from my lunch break. Dressed in my corporate uniform, with a three-piece 1980s suit and a tie, I felt the unmistakable tug of the Holy Spirit on my heart to go to the scene of the accident to pray and to share the gospel with whomever would listen. In that moment, however, I chickened out. "What would people think" became more important to me than what God would think. I shrunk back, went back to work and now more than thirty years later I still cannot forget that scene.

Jesus comes to know hunger and thirst, pain and betrayal and ultimately takes on the fullness of God's eternal wrath against the sins of the world. Jesus absorbs the powerful wrath of a holy God that a million years of torment cannot begin to quench—and He drinks down the cup of God's wrath to its very dregs on the cross of Calvary. And yet I shut my mouth and refuse to witness because someone might think I'm weird! May the Lord have mercy upon my soul.

THE GOSPEL AS THE FUEL OF MISSION

If we come into a true depth of relationship with Jesus (the upward movement) and begin to know ourselves and our desperate need for Christ better (the inward movement), then we are more and more compelled to walk in the footsteps of Jesus (the outward movement). And His footsteps, as we have seen in the Old and New Testaments, are forever moving towards the salvation and redemption of people who are far from Him. The scandalous message of the Scripture is this: "while we were still weak, at the right time Christ died for the ungodly" (Rom. 5:6).

Romans 5:6 proclaims the gospel in a simple but pure form. While we are "still weak" Christ comes for us. The Greek word for weak (*asthenis*) has two primary emphases. Weak can refer to "a state of helplessness in view of circumstances" or to "being morally weak and hence incapable of doing good."[1] Christ comes for those who are helpless and morally corrupt. The last part of the verse tells us that He comes for the "ungodly" (Greek: *asebis*). This word means to be "impious, wicked, ungodly, *i.e.*, pertaining to living without regard for religious belief or practice."[2] We can summarize who Jesus came for this way—He came for pitifully helpless and morally corrupt God-haters!

Do you see that as an accurate description of yourself apart from the work of God in your life? If you do, it is actually a good thing. It means that you agree that Jesus Christ came and died for you! The wonder of the gospel is that when you accept Christ you become a beloved child of God. Your "beloved" status is not based on your performance at all but on the perfect obedience of Jesus whose spotless record has been credited to you. O the depth and the riches of the glorious grace of our great God and King! Praise to You Lord Jesus Christ!

Is this news wonderful to you or do you often kind of take it for granted? I know that much of my Christian life has been one of slumbering on this greatest blessing while living in anxiety and fear about lesser things. The sometimes pathetic pattern that I have noticed in my life is an ungrateful heart, focused on worldly desires, that yawns with malaise and apathy at the wonder of the gospel. I especially notice this when I am living out of my own strength and running on autopilot, oblivious to my own sin. The keen awareness of my own sin, however, leads me to a fresh awareness of the glorious grace of the gospel.

As I grow older I am finding it more and more helpful to confess my sins to God daily and to other people frequently. This practice helps me to cultivate an ongoing awareness of my desperate need for God and a thankfulness for His redeeming work through Jesus Christ. Because confession involves the willful acknowledgment of my sins, it helps to center me in the reality of my ever-present need for Jesus. This leads to the joy, hope and freedom that only serial repenters can know.

So what does all of this have to do with mission? Everything. The fuel for biblical mission is not guilty "I shoulds" uttered by a defeated and fearing soul. No not at all! The fuel for a life marked by missionary engagement is an ongoing awareness of the unspeakably great, loving kindness of God who breaks through every barrier to redeem my lost soul. It is living life saturated in the astonishing reality that Jesus Christ came to save me—even me! And if He has come for me then He has also come for many others and I have been given the privilege of sharing His eternity-changing love with them.

THE EFFECT OF JESUS' LOVE

In Second Corinthians 5:14–15 the apostle Paul put it in these words: "For the love of Christ controls us, because we have concluded this: that one has died for all, therefore all have died; and he died for all, that those who live might no longer live for themselves but for him who for their sake died and was raised." Paul says that the love of Christ "controls us." The core meaning of the Greek word used here (*sunecho*) is to seize something.[3] It is used in the New Testament in various ways.

Luke uses the word for people being seized with great fear (see 8:37), for Jesus being *surrounded* by people (see 8:45), for disciples being *hemmed in* by enemies (see 19:43), and for Jesus being *held in custody* (see 22:63). Paul's only other usage of the word is in Philippians 1:23 when he describes himself as being *hard pressed* to decide whether he should continue to live and do ministry or to depart from this life to be with the Lord. The idea that the Scripture is conveying in Second Corinthians 5:14 is the idea that Paul and his companions are hemmed in or held in custody by the love of God. God's love has so overwhelmed them, through their reflection on the death and resurrection of Jesus, that their behavior and actions are now controlled or determined by their awareness of this amazing love.

What impact does this knowledge have on the behavior of Paul and his companions? This question is answered in verse 20: "Therefore, we are ambassadors for Christ, God making his appeal through us. We implore you on behalf of Christ, be reconciled to God." We see here two critical implications of a life that is seized by the knowledge of God's love. First the fundamental awareness of my identity as a beloved child of God makes me a missionary ambassador. The calling as a missionary ambassador for Christ is an essential element of the Christian identity. This is not merely the identity of those with the gift of evangelism or for clergy or foreign missionaries, but it is foundational for every believer.

Secondly, this identity radically informs my interactions with others around me. "We implore you on behalf of Christ, be reconciled to God." To implore (Greek: *deomai*) means "to ask for with urgency, with the implication of presumed need—to plead or to beg."[4] Paul uses the Greek present tense which means that this is not merely a one-time appeal but the ongoing way in which he and his companions relate to those who do not know Christ. Do you see the passion in these words?

Paul and his companions understand that those they are interacting with desperately need to be reconciled to God through Jesus Christ. They understand that unless they are reconciled they will continue to be without hope and without God in this world (see Eph. 2:12). Furthermore, without reconciliation they will die in their sins (see John 8:24) and be eternally separated from God in hell. This breaks their hearts and compels them (see 2 Cor. 5:14) to make it their urgent and continual plea to call people to Christ (see 5:20).

FUNCTIONAL ATHEISM

I have been greatly convicted by the Holy Spirit of how often I totally fail to care for the plight of lost people. My passion for my favorite team winning a game or my concern for an enhancement to my home can so overwhelm my mind that the reality of people's eternal destinies are pushed to the side. That's crazy right? When this happens I am living as a functional atheist and not as a Christian. I have bought into the value system of this world in such a way that it cannot be said of me that "the love of Christ controls me."

As you honestly look over how you interact with people on a daily basis and what preoccupies your mind, would you say that you struggle with this as well? The good news of the gospel is that when we as "sinner-saints" and believers who are in progress realize this, we can repent and cry out to God to give us a true and lasting change of heart. We can know for sure that when we ask Him for this, God is predisposed to answer this prayer and to move us to a greater and more consistent care for those who do not know Jesus.

A LIFESTYLE OF LOVE

We live in an information-rich society that overwhelms our minds and souls with words, images and messages that we can never hope to really process. Contemporary American culture has been hijacked by the cult of celebrity. This results in ensuring that a great deal of our news, information and entertainment centers around the lives of people who may have a talent or gift for acting, singing or playing a particular sport or be involved in politics or other high profile positions.

Our twenty-four-hour infotainment culture presses into every facet of their lives for mass consumption by the public. We are incessantly informed about their relationships (especially when there is scandal), their clothing choices, their bank accounts, their children, their vacations, and the list goes on and on. This diet of excess about people we don't have any relationship with can easily consume our thoughts and create a virtual world that we believe ourselves to be vitally involved in, but in reality we are merely Peeping Toms who add no value or meaning.

Social networking in all its nuances can have a similar impact. We can easily become lonely and isolated persons with eight hundred virtual "friends." We create virtual personas by selectively sharing our lives online to suggest a version of ourselves that we want others to see and that we actually want to believe in. And in all of this actual relationships, real caring and genuine love are often the casualties. So the Twitterverse hangs on the musings about my latest meal at the newest restaurant in town while my wife wonders why we ever went out to eat in the first place.

Against this tsunami of contrived "reality" there is a core calling for every believer that is based in the very nature of God Himself. "Beloved, let us love one another, for love is from God, and whoever loves has been born of God and knows God. Anyone who does not love does not know God, because God is love" (1 John 4:7–8). The call to love actual people who we are in real relationships with is based upon the fundamental reality of who God is. "God is love." The fact that God is love must set the agenda for how believers live. This demands that we radically de-emphasize our involvement in infotainment and the virtual world in order to focus our lives and efforts on loving the people that God has put in our paths. And that love will consist primarily of one thing—clearly declaring the love of God in Jesus Christ through our words and actions.

In terms of our relationships with those who do not have a saving relationship with Jesus Christ, this means relating to them in such a way that our lives consistently point them to the beauty and wonder of what a relationship with Jesus looks like. I suggest six principles which must be at work if we are to make evangelism a critical priority on our lives:

1. **Committing to a lifestyle of prayer for lost people.** This involves an ongoing commitment to pray for people who do not know Jesus. This commitment to prayer underscores

two critical realities. First, by praying for them we are acknowledging that only God is able to save them. Secondly, by praying for them we are bringing specific individuals before the throne of grace and beseeching God to have mercy on specific people that He has placed in our lives.

2. **Demonstrating practical care for the needs of others.** This means that we assess and act on meeting the practical needs of those we interact with. These are not the deep spiritual needs of others but the basic needs that they are highly aware of. This is as simple as being kind to grocery store clerk who is having a difficult day or leaving a proper tip for a hard-working waitress. This is as difficult as making ongoing personal sacrifices to care for a hurting member of your family or changing your schedule to meet with a friend in crisis. Following in the steps of Jesus, we look to meet the practical needs of those who the Lord puts in our lives.

3. **Paying attention to every interaction.** Perhaps this is as countercultural as anything in our fast-paced and stressed-out world. Being fully present (not preoccupied) in the moment is a gift to others that is more and more rare in our world.

4. **Seeing the greatest need of others in a personal way.** This takes real focus and care for the individual. It is beyond simple clichés such as "Jesus is the answer." In loving the person well, we grow in knowledge of the specific issues, difficulties, temptations and abuses that have played a part in their life formation. This means taking a thoughtful approach to understanding how the call and promise of the gospel intersects with their lives.

5. **Living out a consistent Christian lifestyle.** This does not mean living in the pretense of perfection, but living in the gratitude of God's goodness. The lifestyle of the "sinner-saint"/ "beloved child of God" is one of confession and repentance that others can see. We are able to share our ongoing struggles with others in a way that highlights both the grace of God's forgiveness and the grace of His transformational power which are centered in the person and work of Jesus Christ.
6. **Plainly telling others about Jesus Christ.** One saying that is often quoted by Christians is, "Preach the gospel at all times. Use words if necessary." This is erroneously attributed to Saint Francis of Assisi who apparently never said anything like this.[5] The simple fact is that our actions will never be enough. The gospel is a verbal proclamation of the specific way that God has made provision to forgive sinners through the finished work of Jesus Christ. The need to repent of our sin and accept the death of Christ as the payment for our sin-debt must be communicated in words. Every other item on this list enables us to verbally communicate the gospel with integrity and the help of the Holy Spirit.

And so we see that our outward movement toward others is simply us entering into the activity of God who is always on mission. Every believer in Jesus Christ is called to be on mission for Him. As our culture becomes more and more secularized this is an opportunity to share Christ in a way that shows His uniqueness. Evangelism must never be seen as the job of a select few gifted people. Mature believers share the gospel with people who don't have a relationship with Jesus Christ. In this regard it is ironic that oftentimes the newest "baby" Christians demonstrate more maturity than those who have been saved for decades.

Finally, I want to reaffirm that sharing Christ must not come from cultic tactics that pile on guilt for those who have not met their witnessing quota. If sharing your faith is hard for you, then my first admonition would be for you to go back and look at what you really believe. If Jesus is just of some help to you like a hot cup of coffee on a cold morning, then it is no wonder you do not share to gospel with passion. If you think your sins are not all that bad in comparison to others, then you don't really need the gospel (the blood of Jesus and all that stuff). But if you know that you know that you know that you were surely on your way to hell because of your sin . . . If you know that you resisted God and were rightly called a God-hater . . . If you know that even on your best day you fall short of God's glory—WAAAAY short . . . then perhaps the gospel means more to you.

It is out of the depth of our conscious awareness of the scandalously extravagant love of God that we are blessed to be able to tell others about Jesus. I pray that as you embrace these three movements to make Jesus Christ the center of your life, you will live *in* gratitude and *from* gratitude. I pray that above all else you may know and experience the love of Jesus Christ as you await that blessed day when you will be like Him because you will see Him just as He is (see 1 John 3:2).

To You, O Lord, be honor and glory and majesty. Help me, Lord, to see You in Your splendor and witness the grandeur of Your love and grace. Move me, O God, that my lips may not be silent and that my tongue may not be still. Stir me by the Holy Spirit that I may proclaim the wonders of Jesus to a world without hope.

Overcome my fears and glorify Your name through this body of clay. Use me as Your vessel to tell others of Your immeasurable love that You have demonstrated in Jesus Christ. Move, O God, even through my feeble witness, to save a people for Your own glory. May Your name be glorified in all of these things I pray, in the name of the Father, and of the Son, and of the Holy Spirit. Amen.

CONCLUSION

I freed a thousand slaves. I could have freed a thousand more if only they knew they were slaves.

—Harriet Tubman

We jumped into our huge 1983 dark green hoopty, excited to be on our way from Philadelphia to Florida. As my wife and I helped situate our three young children in the back seat they were eager to be on their way to see family. Sandwiches, fruit, cookies, snacks, drinks and all other necessities were in place as we started the eighteen-hour/two-stops-for-the-bathroom-and-gas trip. Starting up our car, which had been used by the Lord to increase our prayer lives, we began the journey. Everything was mapped out with great precision. Getting our 4:00 a.m. start would have us in the middle of Georgia by 4:00 p.m. and sitting in Tallahassee by 10:00 p.m. All systems go.

All things, however, did not go according to plan. Plan #1 was that the kids would be asleep for the first four hours. But the excitement of the trip had them awake. It did not take long for the inevitable "are we there yets?" and bathroom emergencies to kick in. All of a sudden the two-stop trip was no more.

Plan #2 was that the car would be just fine. Somewhere in the middle of North Carolina our 1983 Buick LeSabre had other plans. New and interesting noises had me concerned and then a sudden loss of power jolted me to attention. We had just enough juice to roll into a rural BP station complete with a dog sitting next to the station owner in his blue overalls while sipping on a Mountain Dew. We were relieved not to be stuck on the highway but a little concerned with how things were going. As they put us on top of a flatbed tow truck with all the kids in the car I knew that this was not in the plan.

Eventually—literally a day late and a few dollars short—we ended up at our destination. Had someone told me in advance what the journey would entail I definitely would have decided on a staycation. All the hassle, the money and the lost time were not in the plan or the budget. But, to be honest, once we got there our vacation was wonderful.

This little vignette reminds me a great deal of my journey to know Christ well. Very few things have gone the way I planned or expected. The frustrations along the way have been many and my progress has been much slower than I had originally anticipated. My "two-stop trip" has ended up with more stops than I can count. On numerous occasions God has graciously shown me that I was not where I thought I was in terms of my maturity in Christ.

EMBRACING THE JOURNEY

On the journey to make Jesus the center of my life I have noticed my strong tendency to make this a very complicated thing. The more I grow in Him, however, I am convinced that this is not that complicated after all. Of course, it is hard, but it is not complicated. It requires the simple willingness to put fleshly desires to death and resist the matrix that the world offers for pseudo happiness, peace and joy. This is done not by my strength but by the power of God at work in me through the truth of the gospel. In relation to knowing life in Jesus I have often been like the many slaves that Harriet Tubman spoke of. Many, she said, couldn't be set free because they were unaware that they were slaves. Only by God's grace have I been able to see the slavery and bondage that God is leading me out of. Through Word, Spirit and Christian community, God is at work taking the blinders off my eyes to see the true simplicity of life in Jesus.

Here is the most basic of all Christian propositions: Life is in Jesus—period. Here is the most troubling and stubborn statement of the reality of daily life for most Christians: I am looking for life apart from Jesus. The gap between the proposition, or doctrine, and the statement of reality has been the subject of this book. Making that statement less and less true, or positively stated, living a life where Jesus Christ is more consistently made the central value, affection and pursuit of my life is the God-desired end of every Christian life.

Nothing in the pages of this book proposes a magic pill or some easy, quick fix to make Jesus-centeredness the consistent reality of your life. I have found this to be long, hard and slow work. However, a conscious awareness of each of the three movements accompanied by a diligent pursuit of each promises great rewards. By recognizing your need for the upward, inward and outward movements, and giving your attention to each, you will find Jesus encroaching on every area of your life. This is the encroachment of the loving and perfect Savior who comes to offer real life, true peace, and living communion with God.

Jesus encroaches on your relationships. Jesus encroaches on your work and academic pursuits. Jesus encroaches on how you interact with others in the grocery store, on the bus or even driving in traffic. There is no place, no relationship, no time and no sphere of life to which Jesus will ever take a hands-off approach. He concerns Himself with every area of your life for two reasons: His glory and your good.

LIVING FOR GOD'S GLORY

It is extremely important to be aware that the primary reason for all of this is that God might be glorified. As creator, sustainer, redeemer, and Lord over time and eternity we must acknowledge that we exist for God alone. He has exclusive rights over us and we exist as a part of a universe designed by Him to bring glory to Him. *Most of what slows us down in our Christian growth is our refusal to make our lives about Jesus rather than ourselves.* Making our lives about Jesus does not mean that we lose our sense of self, stop enjoying pleasures, or no longer pursue goals. Making our lives about Jesus means that our primary goal becomes knowing Him better and bringing glory and honor to His name. Making our lives about Jesus means that our identity is found in our union with Christ. The willingness to joyfully embrace making our lives about Jesus is the key paradigmatic shift that allows believers to truly grow as disciples.

An unwillingness to embrace this shift underlies the thinking of most of those who end up leaving the church and breaking away from Christian community. One of the most difficult things I have experienced as a believer is seeing people I love walk away from God. Many of them appeared at one time to have a strong and emotionally intense relationship with Jesus. However, at some point they made conscious decisions to reject God as He has revealed Himself in the Bible. The stubborn refusal to make their lives about Jesus leads them to search for satisfaction and life apart from Him.

To enhance their self-esteem they deny their sin and therefore break off the cycle of confession, repentance, forgiveness and restoration that is the lifeblood of Christian growth. Although they may still claim Jesus as their own, they have left the Jesus of the Bible for a Jesus of their own imagination. Seeing this happen to people I love over the years has been a great cause of sorrow.

I grieve deeply for the many who are looking to a Jesus that exists only as a figment of their imagination. He does not require repentance, and He does not make life about His glory. My great hope and prayer is that many who have been deceived in this way will see Jesus as He is portrayed in Scripture and recognize that He is their only true hope. Only when we recognize that the purpose of our lives is to glorify Jesus can we experience the true freedom of what it means to experience life as a child of the living God (see Rom. 8:15–17).

HOW THE MOVEMENTS WORK TOGETHER

How do each of these three movements work together to produce healthy, growing disciples? Centering the daily rhythms of your life on being consciously aware of Jesus' presence is the essence of the first movement—the upward movement. Making this the first priority of your life, you find yourself gradually escaping the illusion of autonomy that is so powerfully engraved upon your flesh. As you begin to grow in "practicing the presence of God" (to use the famous phrase from the seventeenth-century French monk, Brother Lawrence) your awareness of Jesus' presence brings both peace and challenge. Gospel awareness gives you the peace of knowing that you are a beloved child while at the same time you are being radically challenged to become conformed to His image. God lovingly and skillfully cuts you with His divine pruning shears to realign the attitudes and motivations of your heart to be in line with His.

In this work of realignment everything about your self-understanding is eventually challenged and changed. This is the second movement—the inward movement. Like a chiropractor bringing vertebrae into proper alignment so that nerves work properly without interference, God adjusts your identity by challenging you to apply the gospel to every crack and crevice of your soul. Life in Jesus does not mean that Jesus is the GPS that enables you to reach a destination called "life," but that Jesus is the destination in which life is found—Jesus Life! Tearing down every false identity that allows you to find meaning and purpose apart from Jesus, the inward journey then reconstructs every part of your life around right relationship with Jesus. The inward journey moves you from a sometimes blissful but ultimately deadly numbness of God's claim on your life, to a conscious awareness of His rightful place as Lord over all.

The implications of this begin to saturate every part of your soul and call for a drastic change in how you relate to others. This is the third and final movement—the outward movement. This is simply the proper application of the new reality that you have begun to grasp in the first two movements. The fact that Jesus is here—right here and right now—calls you to live out every relationship in light of that reality. This call is to true love, not the sappy, feelings-based drivel that is so often passed off as love. The call is to love others as God has loved you. To pursue others hard with grace and truth. To know and to be known. To never be content with false peace. To understand that you are your brother's keeper and that you are called to a radical lifestyle of love and care for others. To pray for and to engage those who do not even understand their need for God and urge them to come to Jesus who is the only source of life.

Jesus promised that "whoever loses his life for my sake will find it" (Matt. 10:39). This is the result of life consciously lived in Jesus' presence and for His glory. This never becomes a hyper-spiritual form of religion that leads to pride, but instead becomes an intensely practical way of walking in humility with God and among brothers and sisters. The ongoing awareness of each of these movements leads us to be grateful people who are growing to appreciate salvation more and more as the degree of our brokenness is revealed and the depth of God's love towards us is consistently manifested.

FINAL WORDS

These three movements come together to form a life centered on Jesus Christ. This life is not empowered by tricks, gizmos, or fads but by the indestructible power of the gospel. We are moved to live a life increasingly informed by the reality proclaimed in the memorial acclamation, "Christ has died, Christ is risen, Christ will come again."[1] We make Jesus the goal of our lives and not the means to an end.

I pray that this book will help you grow closer to Jesus. I am sure that you will have seasons of testing and trial and times of refreshing and peace. My prayer is that with every unexpected and difficult trial, and with every pleasant and wonderful blessing, you will be increasingly aware of the abiding presence of Jesus. May you glory in the strong love of the only One who is able to save and deliver you. I pray that your life will become a living epistle pointing with increasing consistency to Jesus. May you experience on earth a taste of that which you are being prepared for in eternity—Jesus Life.

Psalm 73:23–28
A Psalm of Asaph

Nevertheless, I am continually with you;
  you hold my right hand.
You guide me with your counsel,
  and afterward you will receive me to glory.
Whom have I in heaven but you?
  And there is nothing on earth that
  I desire besides you.
My flesh and my heart may fail,
  but God is the strength of my heart
  and my portion forever.
For behold, those who are far from you shall perish;
  you put an end to everyone
  who is unfaithful to you.
But for me it is good to be near God;
  I have made the Lord GOD my refuge,
  that I may tell of all your works.

Appendix 1

THE JESUS PRAYER

Lord Jesus Christ, Son of God, have mercy on me a sinner.

—Ancient Prayer

There is a long tradition of contemplative prayer in the church which has been formulated in what it known as the Jesus Prayer. Some estimate that this form of prayer goes back as far as the third to fifth centuries as it was practiced by the Desert Fathers.[1] This prayer became very popular among the Eastern Orthodox but has at times also been used by Catholics and more recently by Protestants as well.

The basic formula of the prayer is this: "Lord Jesus Christ, Son of God, have mercy on me a sinner." The idea of the prayer comes out of the cry of the tax collector in Luke 18:13 who, aware of the depth of his sin, prays to God by saying, "God, be merciful to me, a sinner!" This is in stark contrast to the Pharisee who is haughty and boastful in his prayer and thanks God that he is not like other men. The posture of the prayer is one of humility and thankfulness. Jesus concludes His teaching in Luke 18:14 by saying of the tax collector, "I tell you, this man went down to his house justified, rather than the other. For everyone who exalts himself will be humbled, but the one who humbles himself will be exalted."

I began to use this prayer in my own life as a means of increasing my awareness of the presence of God during the day. Some use this prayer by consistently chanting it over and over again but I do not see scriptural warrant for this (see Matt. 6:7–8). Thoughtfully and slowing saying this prayer was helpful for me to get my mind centered on Jesus, to be aware of my need for Him, and to be thankful for what He has done for me.

As I continued doing this, however, I felt that I needed to have something else in this prayer. Humility and thankfulness are essential but I need some help today to overcome my flesh and live for Jesus! With this in mind I added two additional lines to the prayer. The form that I use now looks like this:

> Lord Jesus Christ, Son of God,
>   have mercy on me, a sinner.
> Lord Jesus Christ, Savior of the World,
>   strengthen me to walk with You today.
> Lord Jesus Christ, King of Glory,
>   receive my worship.

I have been using this prayer for some time now and I find it very helpful. The second line builds on thankfulness to include the idea of supplication in asking the Lord for strength to live for Him. In this line I remember Jesus as the Savior who not only forgives sin but also empowers His people to resist sin. I am calling on His name to give me victory today against the world, the flesh and the devil that conspire draw me away from God.

The final line is both eschatological and practical. The title, King of Glory, hearkens back to the refrain of Psalm 24. Jesus is revealed as the King of Glory who is the Lord of hosts. He is the one who is the Lord, strong and mighty. Jesus is the undisputed Lord of the universe who alone is worthy of worship. To

Him alone I bow down and offer my life as a living sacrifice, which is my reasonable service of worship (see Rom. 12:1).

One way I understand this threefold prayer is seeing it as moving from thankfulness for justification, to supplication for sanctification, to petition for glorification. In our glorified state our worship will be perfected. The third stanza reminds me, however, that all of my life—even now—is viewed by God as worship. It is either true worship to the true God or it is idolatry. Whether that idol is sex, greed, money, success, man-pleasing or any of hundreds of other options, is of little consequence. As I pray, I am brought back to a sober awareness of my place before Almighty God. Can I call what I have been doing in the last hour worship? Will I live the next hour of my life, whether at work, at home, in my car, shopping or enjoying recreation, in a way that reflects intentional worship of Jesus Christ?

I repeat this prayer slowly and thoughtfully several times during the day. Usually I will pause after each line to reflect on what I have just said. Sometimes I say the prayer out loud and sometimes I repeat it silently. Most days I will pray this before I get out of bed. I use this to help me keep Jesus at the center of my thoughts and to help orient my actions to reflect my relationship with Him. This has proven to be a useful tool for me in my quest to live a more consistently Christ-centered life.

Of course this all comes with a word of warning. There is no prayer or practice that somehow has magical qualities that automatically makes one more devoted to Christ. God is always dealing with the disposition of our hearts. This prayer is one tool among many for me to reflect on the disposition of my heart and adjust my mind and heart more to the frequency of Jesus.

I encourage you to incorporate this prayer into your life. You may want to write it down at first so that you can pull it out at any time during the day and recite it. It should not take long to memorize it. The idea is to allow your recitation of the prayer to consciously focus your attention on Jesus. The movement of each line allows you to reflect on different aspects of Jesus in His relationship to you with the effect of moving you to worship. I have found that using this prayer consistently during busy times in the day can help me to slow down and experience the presence of Jesus when it is otherwise easy to get caught up in busyness and lose the awareness of God's presence. I pray that this prayer can be helpful in keeping your life centered on Jesus.

Appendix 2

GOSPEL-BASED

DNA Groups

Discipleship – Nurture – Accountability[1]

Only let your manner of life be worthy of the gospel of Christ, so that whether I come and see you or am absent, I may hear of you that you are standing firm in one spirit, with one mind striving side by side for the faith of the gospel.

Philippians 1:27

THE PURPOSE AND PRACTICE OF GOSPEL-BASED DNA GROUPS

Gospel-Based DNA Groups are clusters of two or three believers of the same gender who are committed to coming together regularly to grow in Christ. Most often they will come together on a weekly basis. There are three purposes and three corresponding practices that fuel their growth:

PURPOSES	PRACTICES
1. Knowing My God	Meditation on Scripture
2. Knowing My Sin	Introspection/Confession
3. Trusting My Savior	Edification/Affirmation

1. Knowing My God

Growing in Christ is intimately related to knowing Christ. To know deeply is to grow deeply. *Too often Christian accountability groups set up to help people overcome sin, focus so much on sin that Christ's transforming power is missed.* To "see him as he is" (1 John 3:2) is to be transformed into His glorious image. Due to this dynamic, the first portion of a Gospel-Based DNA Group meeting is to meditate on some aspect of God as He has revealed Himself in Scripture.

Group members agree to meditate on a certain Scripture passage and share with one another the insights they have gained. This is not a subjective "what I think this passage means to me is . . . " session. This is a time of focusing on how God reveals Himself in His word. Some questions to come to the Scripture with that may be helpful are:

- What attribute of God is highlighted in this passage?
- How do I clearly see Christ's saving purpose revealed in this passage?
- How is God calling me to obedience through this passage?

Because the primary purpose of Gospel-Based DNA Groups is to help believers grow in their knowledge and trust of God, this part of the meeting is very important. *Apart from a right understanding of God and the good news of the gospel, we will never have the freedom to look at and expose our sin.* When we grasp the gospel truth that our right standing with God is totally based upon the righteousness of Jesus Christ, we no longer have to justify ourselves, minimize our sin or otherwise try to make ourselves look good. The Father accepts us because the righteousness of the Son was applied to our lives by the work of the Spirit. Our great God has freely given us grace beyond what we could ever hope for or imagine! To know Him more intimately allows us to confidently "draw near to the throne of grace, that we may receive mercy and find grace to help in time of need" (Heb. 4:16).

2. Knowing My Sin

With their eyes clearly set on the beauty of the Savior, group members can now confess areas of sin and disobedience in their lives to one another. This may be prompted specifically by something in the passage or may be more generally dealing with ongoing areas that they need to mature in. Growing in honesty and transparency through confession is critical to growing in Christ. The original pattern of sin displayed in Genesis 3 is a three-step process of disobedience, hiding and blameshifting. *Here, by the freeing power of the gospel, group members replace hiding and blameshifting with confession and repentance.* Our flesh and the Enemy of our souls will confront each person at this point to continue the pattern of hiding and blameshifting. As group members we must encourage one another by example and exhortation to an honest confession of our sin.

Maturing Christians grow in the awareness of their sin. The closer a person grows to Christ, the more they see how the motivations and intentions of their heart are self-centered and ungodly. By growing in our knowledge of God, we are enabled to deal with sin more comprehensively. It is important for group members not only to look at certain actions of sin (sexual issues, lying, anger, unkindness), but also deal with heart issues (pride, idolatry, hypocrisy, self-centeredness, etc.). Group members expose their sin to one another and bring it to Christ in a spirit of repentance. Confession of sin should be specific and honest.

3. Trusting My Savior

True repentance is not found in just confession or sorrow over sin (see 2 Cor. 7:10) but in turning away from sin and to Christ. One Greek word often used in the New Testament for repentance is *metanoia*. This word means a change of mind or purpose.[2] In essence this means to change my direction from the path that leads to sin, to the path that leads to Christ. Repentance demands both an honest confession of sin and a change of direction empowered by trusting in Jesus.

We sin because we get something out of it that we like. It may be momentary pleasure, it may be position or status or it may be a temporary escape from the difficulties of life. Sin heals us. Sin heals our wounds for a time and makes us feel better for a little while. But sin only heals on the surface (see Jer. 8:11). Sin allows the nagging issues of life that drive us to it to grow and flourish in such a way that they eventually overcome and destroy us. Sin works like a Band-Aid on a cancerous tumor. For a little while the tumor is covered and we feel better, but nothing has been done to really heal it.

The gospel allows us to deal with the tumor of sin in truth, and trust Jesus Christ for the healing. We don't have to be afraid to look at it in all its ugliness. He died to forgive us of it, He lives in us to overcome it and He is coming again to totally destroy it! We are able to say triumphantly with the apostle Paul, "O death, where is your victory? O death, where is your sting? The sting of death is sin, and the power of sin is in the law. But thanks be to God, who gives us victory through our Lord Jesus Christ" (1 Cor. 15:55–57).

The last part of the Gospel-Based DNA Group meeting is encouraging one another to trust Jesus fully in repenting from sin. This is a time of encouraging and praying earnestly for one another. As the group members look away from sin and from self to Jesus, they are empowered by the Holy Spirit to experience and live out a deep and true repentance. *Group members patiently and lovingly point each other to Jesus in their heartfelt desire to be conformed more and more to His image.*

It is important to remember that success in a Gospel-Based DNA Group is not defined by the total eradication of sin—that will not happen while we inhabit our mortal bodies. The goal is to see the light of Christ more clearly against the background of our sin and therefore be progressively transformed by His grace. *Legalism has no place here. Gospel transformation happens as the by-product of seeing and believing in God's unfathomable love that was perfectly portrayed in the life, death and resurrection of Jesus Christ.* Seeing Jesus more clearly and coming to grasp the staggering reality of the furious love of the triune God produces the by-product of deep and true repentance. *As we "taste and see that the Lord is good"* (Ps. 34:8) *we see our sin for what it is—a futile attempt to find satisfaction apart from the only One who is capable of satisfying our thirsty souls.*

Seeing God more clearly also calls us to spend time praying specifically for people in each members life who are not yet following Christ. The end of God's sanctifying work in a believer is not simply that they look better, but that Christ is more powerfully manifested in and through their lives. *To this end, sanctification always fuels gospel mission.*

SUMMARY

Gospel-Based DNA Groups are a powerful way to help a community of believers to mature in Christ. Within the context of a church community that faithfully preaches the Word of God, Gospel-Based DNA Groups allow small clusters of two or three believers to point one another to Christ, expose sin, and allow God to purify them. Because of the degree to which the members confess their sins these groups, they must always be of the same gender. Keeping the groups to two or three persons allows for frequent contact and a depth of relationship that will not be possible with larger groups.

Forming these groups takes a significant commitment from each member. Members covenant to do the following:

- Meet in person regularly (weekly or at least once every two weeks).
- Read and meditate on God's Word regularly.
- Honestly expose their own sin.
- Keep in complete confidence what each member reveals.
- Encourage one another to take practical steps to break patterns of sin.
- Pray earnestly for one another to embrace Christ in deep repentance.
- Continually pray for friends, family members and others who are not yet following Christ.

Meetings should last from sixty to ninety minutes. Each meeting should begin with reading and meditating on the Scripture together but should not become primarily a Bible study. This meeting is not a time to eloquently reveal a person's depth of theological knowledge. *It is a time to come broken before a holy God and receive the healing that only He can bring through His Word, His Spirit and His people.*

Gospel-Based DNA Groups work best in concert with other community-based small groups intended to grow body life within the church. Gospel-Based DNA Groups are not regulated or tracked by the church but are encouraged and given resources to help them thrive. Believers who embrace this level of community greatly enhance their ability to grow in Christ, overcome sin and maximize the degree to which Jesus Christ is glorified in and through their lives.

A FINAL WORD

Do you see the need for the level of depth of relationship that a Gospel-Based DNA Group can provide? If we are not purposeful, our relationships have a strong tendency to serve our own comfort. Committing to a long-term DNA group relationship will not always be comfortable—but it will be impactful. This type of commitment, to your own transformation and that of your partner(s) will help you to give Jesus Christ His rightful place as Lord of your life on a more consistent basis. For those who desire to see Jesus Life manifested in their lives, walking with others in this deep level of relationship is indispensable.

NOTES

Part One: The Upward Movement

Finding Life by Connecting to Jesus

1. D.A. Carson, *Basics for Believers: An Exposition of Philippians.* (Grand Rapids: Baker Academic, 1996), 12-13.

Chapter 2: Developing a Longing to Know Jesus

1. David L. Cook, *Seven Days in Utopia*. (Grand Rapids: Zondervan, 2011).
2. F. Brown, S.R. Driver and C.A. Briggs, *Enhanced Brown-Driver-Briggs Hebrew and English Lexicon* (Oak Harbor, WA: Logos Research Systems, 2000).
3. T. Adeyemo, *African Bible Commentary.*(Nairobi: WordAlive Publishers, Zondervan, 2006), 639.
4. *NET Bible®*, (Biblical Studies Press, L.L.C.: copyright ©1996-2006), Psalm 84:11 notes.
5. Oswald Chambers, *My Utmost for His Highest: An Updated Edition in Today's Language, The Golden Book of Oswald Chambers,* ed. James Reimann. (Grand Rapids: Discovery House Publishers, 1992). page for July 30.There is a positive and good understanding of disillusionment as well. Oswald Chambers speaks of disillusionment as that which takes away our misconceptions about life and people in such a way that we have a realistic view of them. Chambers says, "But the disillusionment that comes from

God brings us to the point where we see people as they really are, yet without any cynicism or any stinging and bitter criticism." This is only possible if disillusionment is accompanied by a love for God and for truth and a rejection of the ethos of entitlement.

6. This does not mean that we deny the hardships of life or refuse to grieve our losses. The Bible never calls believers to deny our grief but it does call us to grieve in a way that that is rooted in the hope of the gospel (see 1 Thess. 4:13). In the midst of a believer's grief there is sure hope, based on the historical acts and the consistent character of God, that He is in the process of redeeming all things for the purpose of His glory and our good. This bedrock belief makes even the grief of believers markedly different from that of unbelievers and leaves room for thankfulness and gratitude even in the most seemingly hopeless situations.

Chapter 3: Stopping to Be With Jesus

1. J.P Louw and E.A. Nida, *Greek-English Lexicon of the New Testament: Based on Semantic Domains*. (New York: United Bible Societies, 1996).
2. M.G. Easton, *Easton's Bible Dictionary* New York: Harper & Brothers, 1893. (electronic ed. Oak Harbor, WA: Logos Research Systems, 2000), "Gehenna".
3. D.A. Carson, "Matthew" in *The Expositor's Bible Commentary: Matthew, Mark, Luke,* Vol. 8, ed. F. E. Gaebelein. (Grand Rapids: Zondervan Publishing House, 1984), 186.
4. Ibid.

5. Peter Scazzero, *Emotionally Healthy Spirituality*. (Nashville: Zondervan, 2006), 153–74.
6. Timothy Fry, ed., *The Rule of Saint Benedict.* (New York: Random House, 1998), xv.
7. Scazzero, *Emotionally Healthy Spirituality,* 153–174.

Chapter 4: Moving Forward in Jesus

1. *Napoleon Dynamite,* directed by Jared Hess, 2004; Preston and Franklin, ID: Fox Searchlight Pictures, film.
2. Brown, Driver and Briggs, Enhanced Brown-Driver-Briggs Hebrew and English Lexicon (electronic ed. Oak Harbor, WA: Logo Research Systems).
3. Ibid. (electronic ed., p. 944)
4. John Mason, "I've Found the Pearl of Greatest Price," 1683.
5. Brown, Driver and Briggs, (2000). *Enhanced Brown-Driver-Briggs Hebrew and English Lexicon* (electronic ed., p. 772. Oak Harbor, WA: Logos Research Systems).
6. Louw and Nida, *Greek-English Lexicon of the New Testament: Based on Semantic Domains, (electronic ed. of the 2nd edition,* Vol 1, p. 473. New York: United Bible Societies).
7. Thomas Chalmers, "The Expulsive Power of a New Affection," Sermon listed on SermonIndex.net on August 30, 2003. Online at http://www.sermonindex.net/modules/newbb/viewtopic.php?topic_id=25002&forum=45.
8. *Napoleon Dynamite,* Hess.

Chapter 5: Life Empowered by the Holy Spirit

1. William Ernest Henley, *A Book of Verses* (London: D. Nutt, 1888), 56.
2. Ibid, pp. 56-57.
3. Edward Mote, "My Hope Is Built on Nothing Less," 1834.
4. William Carl Placher, *Readings in the History of Christian Theology, Volume 1: From Its Beginnings to the Eve of the Reformation* (Philadelphia, PA: Westminster Press, 1988), 52–53. The Nicene Creed is one of the oldest creeds in Christendom. The creed was formulated at the first great ecumenical church council in Nicea in 325 AD. It has been used widely throughout the church for almost seventeen hundred years as a statement of Christian orthodoxy.

Chapter 6: Life Submitted to the Word of God

1. R. Earle, "2 Timothy," in *The Expositor's Bible Commentary: Ephesians through Philemon,* Vol. 11, ed. F. E. Gaebelein, (Grand Rapids: Zondervan Publishing House, 1981), 409.
2. Matt Slick, "Manuscript evidence for superior New Testament reliability," Christian Apologetics and Research Ministry website. Online at www.carm.org/manuscript-evidence.
3. Ibid.
4. Ibid.
5. This information is from the website of the organization Answering Islam. The webpage is http://www.answering-islam.org/Quran/Text/index.html.

6. Matt Slick, "Differences between the Bible and Qur'an," Christian Apologetics and Research Ministry website. Online at https://carm.org/differences-between-bible-and-quran.
7. Bruce, F. F. (1996). Bible. In D. R. W. Wood, I. H. Marshall, A. R. Millard, J. I. Packer, & D. J. Wiseman (Eds.), *New Bible Dictionary* (3rd ed., p. 137). Leicester, England; Downers Grove, IL: InterVarsity Press.
8. "Mormon Book of Problems," Mormon Think website. Online at www.mormonthink.com/book-of-mormon-problems.htm.
9. Merriam-Webster OnLine, s.v. "canon," accessed March 16, 2015, http://www.merriam-webster.com/dictionary/canon.

Chapter 7: Christian Identity Confusion

1. Anthony Hoekema, *Saved by Grace (*Grand Rapids: Wm. B. Eerdmans, 1989). This book is where I first came across this teaching. It is an excellent systematic introduction to how God works in our lives to save us.
2. Horatio Spafford, "It Is Well with My Soul," Gospel Songs No. 2 (Sankey and Bliss, 1876).
3. This is a quote from Winston Churchill on a radio broadcast in 1939. He was asked what role Russia might play in World War II. Quoted from The Phrase Finder website. Online at http://www.phrases.org.uk/meanings/31000.html.

Chapter 8: Three Elements of a Christ-Centered Identity

1. Herman Bavink, *Reformed Dogmatics,* Volume II (Grand Rapids: Baker Academics, a division of Baker Book Company, 2008), 176.
2. This is not meant to be gender-biased language but to mirror the language and thought of the scriptures. In both the ancient Near East and in the first-century Roman Empire, it was the first-born son who had the special rights of inheritance in the family. This is true of every believer in Christ regardless of gender.
3. This scripture is a part of Isaiah's prophetic taunt against the king of Babylon. Many interpreters see this as a typological description of the pride of Satan that led to his being banished from heaven. Jesus speaks of this in Luke 10:18.
4. This is not to imply that gifted people in the church or elsewhere will not be recognized or singled out. In fact it is clear that many great churches are led by called and gifted leaders whose particular skill set is used by God to attract many to the church. The mark of humility, however, is that such a leader is constantly pointing others to Christ and does not make themselves out to be something that they are not. They are able to communicate their brokenness appropriately and lift up Jesus as their one and only great hope.
5. This comment reflects the biblical assertion that man, in distinction from all other created beings, was made in the image and likeness of God. The author recognizes, however, that the distinction between creature and creator is an infinite gulf. Although mankind reflects

those attributes of God that are communicable, such as love, justice and holiness, God possesses every attribute in infinite perfection while mankind possesses these attributes in a diluted fashion mixed with the passions of the sinful nature. Although mankind in the original creation had no imperfection, time and providence revealed a weakness in the will of man as he chose to willingly disobey God in Genesis 3. The redemption story is God's story of bringing man into the eternal destiny that God originally designed for him which ultimately displays God's glory through His justice and mercy in a way which astounds even the angels themselves.

Chapter 10: Loving Christian Community

1. Dietrich Bonhoeffer, *Life Together: The Classic Exploration of Faith in Community* (New York: Harper and Rowe, 1954), 36.
2. "Giant Sequoia Questions," giant-sequoia.com website. Online at http://www.giant-sequoia.com/faqs/giant-sequoia-questions/.
3. "Giant Sequoias," Kingdom Arising Outreach website. Online at http://kingdomarising.org/giant-redwoods.html.
4. "Giant Sequoia Questions," giant-sequoia.com website. Online at http://www.giant-sequoia.com/faqs/giant-sequoia-questions/.
5. Ibid.
6. Ibid.
7. Scazzero, *Emotionally Healthy Spirituality.* I was first introduced to this terminology in the aforementioned book.

8. Louw and Nida, *Greek-English Lexicon of the New Testament: Based on Semantic Domains.*
9. This is not an exact quote but a paraphrase from both sermons and informal conversations with Dr. Mason.
10. "Life Groups," Epiphany Fellowship Church website. Online at http://epiphanyfellowship.org/connect/#post-life-groups.
11. Lawrence Smith, *Gospel-Based DNA Groups,* Epiphany Fellowship Church Philadelphia, PA: 2011.
12. Ken Sande, *The Peacemaker* (Grand Rapids,: Baker Books, 2004).

Chapter 11: Compelled to Tell

1. Swanson, J. (1997). Dictionary of Biblical Languages with Semantic Domains: Greek (New Testament) (electronic ed.). Oak Harbor: Logos Research Systems, Inc., "asthenes".2.
2. Swanson, J. (1997). Dictionary of Biblical Languages with Semantic Domains: Greek (New Testament) (electronic ed.). Oak Harbor: Logos Research Systems, Inc., "asebes".
3. Louw and Nida, *Greek-English lexicon of the New Testament: Based on Semantic Domains.*
4. Ibid, p.407.
5. Glenn T. Stanton, "Factchecker: Misquoting Francis of Assisi," on July 10, 2012 on The Gospel Coalition website. Online http://thegospelcoalition.org/blogs/tgc/2012/07/11/factchecker-misquoting-francis-of-assisi/. Francis of Assisi (1181–1226) was apparently a powerful and animated preacher who spoke up to five

times a day and called people to devotion to Christ. He believed strongly that the preacher should live a life of devotion to Christ that would fuel his passion to share Jesus love with others.

Conclusion

1. Don S. Armentrout and Robert Boak Slocum, eds., *An Episcopal Dictionary of the Church* (New York: Church House Publishing, 2005), 328.

Appendix 1: The Jesus Prayer

1. "The Jesus Prayer," The Jesus Prayer website. Online at http://www.thejesusprayer.net/.

Appendix 2: Gospel-Based DNA Groups

1. Lawrence Smith, *Gospel-Based DNA Groups.*
2. Louw, J. P., & Nida, E. A. (1996). Greek-English Lexicon of the New Testament: based on semantic domains (electronic ed. of the 2nd edition., Vol. 1, p. 509). New York: United Bible Societies.

CLC PUBLICATIONS
Fort Washington, PA 19034

This book is published by CLC Publications, an outreach of CLC Ministries International. The purpose of CLC is to make evangelical Christian literature available to all nations so that people may come to faith and maturity in the Lord Jesus Christ. We hope this book has been life-changing and has enriched your walk with God through the work of the Holy Spirit. If you would like to know more about CLC, we invite you to visit our website:
www.clcusa.org

To know more about the remarkable story of the founding of CLC International we encourage you to read

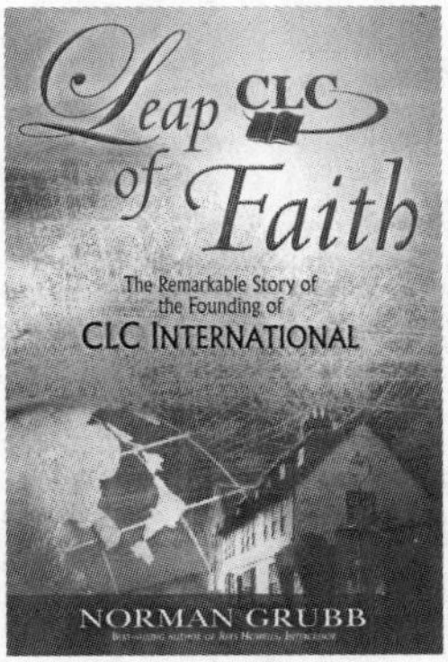

LEAP OF FAITH

Norman Grubb

Paperback
Size 5 1/4 x 8, Pages 248
ISBN: 978-0-87508-650-7
ISBN (*e-book*): 978-1-61958-055-8